Happy Dog, Happy You

A Dog Parenting Handbook

FROM THE PUBLISHERS OF GOOD DOG MAGAZINE

MARGARITA CARPIO, DVM
JOJO ISORENA, DOG TRAINING AND BEHAVIOR SPECIALIST

TABLE OF CONTENTS

Happy Dog, Happy You

A Dog Parenting Handbook

BOOK TEAM

Maggie Adan
Editor

Mikke Gallardo
Art Director

Anna Loraine Balita-Centeno
Managing Editor

Lynn Lopez
Grace Marcellana
Editors at Large

Summit Books is the book publishing division under Summit Media. Summit Books is committed to providing the public with reasonably priced, quality, contemporary books. Its vision is to get Filipinos in the habit of buying and reading books and to do for books what Summit Media has done for magazines.

Summit Books are published by Summit Publishing Co., Inc., a division of Summit Media, 6F & 7F Robinsons Cybergate Tower 3, Robinsons Pioneer Complex Pioneer St., Mandaluyong City 1550

Cover photo by Christian Halili

President
Lisa Gokongwei Cheng

Publisher
Aurora Mangubat Suarez

Team Publisher
Christine Ko

Senior Publishing Assistant
Bianca Romero

Group Advertising Director
Florence Bienvenido

Production Director
Intet Victoriano

Production Coordinator
Dina Jesuitas

Production Artist
JL Patulan

Circulation Manager
Alma Madelo

Deputy National Circulation Manager
Glenda Gil

ABOUT THE AUTHORS

Dr. Marga Carpio graduated in 2000 from the University of the Philippines, Los Baños with a Doctor of Veterinary Medicine degree. She trained in New York and Maryland for two years after graduation before working as the chief veterinarian at the Avilon Zoological Park in Montalban, Rizal.

In 2003, along with three other partners, she opened Vets In Practice (VIP) Animal Hospital in Mandaluyong. In 2009, they moved VIP to its new home along the Mandaluyong Circle and put up the largest veterinary hospital in Metro Manila. In addition to practicing dog, cat, and exotic animal medicine, Dr. Carpio writes a regular column for Summit Media's *Good Dog* magazine. She also works as the magazine's consultant.

Dr. Carpio has special interest and training in holistic approaches to treating common pet ailments. Modalities include Reiki, BioEnergy Therapy, acupuncture, acupressure, and massage therapy. In 2010, she put up the VIP Pet Hotel and Wellness Center in Mandaluyong City.

She shares her heart and home with her husband Nick, daughter Roxie (plus a baby on the way), five dogs, two cats, a tortoise, and a horse.

Jojo Isorena received his certification as a Canine Training and Behavior Specialist at the Triple Crown Academy for Professional Dog Trainers in 2006 where he trained under top professionals and competitors in the field. Upon successfully completing the graduation requirements, he returned to Manila and worked as a vet-referred dog behavior counselor and trainer. In 2009, he and his wife Tina established BetterDog Canine Behavior Center in Makati, the first professional training facility in the Philippines that educates pet owners on teaching their dogs through reward-based methods. Jojo currently lives with wife Tina, their two sons, and 12 dogs, including Fudge, an anxious German Shorthaired Pointer and Prince, a neurotic border collie.

INTRODUCTION

There's a lot more involved—or at least there should be—to getting a dog than just making a trip to the shelter, the breeder, or the pet store, picking the cutest pup in the lot, and taking it home. As a responsible pet parent, you should have carefully thought about your decision, done your research, and prepared yourself and your home before welcoming a canine companion into your life.

Are you ready for a dog? Has your home been puppy-proofed? Do you have the essentials ready—food, crate, tools, equipment, etc.? What kind of dog should you get? Where should you get a dog? There are so many questions you will have to ask yourself and it can seem like such a daunting task. But it doesn't have to be.

The people behind *Good Dog* magazine have come up with this comprehensive guide on dog parenting. Dog behaviorist and trainer Jojo Isorena and Margarita Carpio, D.V.M, two of the country's leading dog experts, share their insights and knowledge in order to prepare and help you become a better dog parent.

Dogs are the only creatures in this world born with the capacity for unconditional love. It is only right that we return their devotion the best way we can—by striving to be responsible dog parents.

CHAPTER 1

Getting Your First Puppy

Whether you are a first-time dog owner or adding another dog to your family, the promise of a new puppy is always held with great excitement and anticipation. A dog, after all, is capable of giving you unconditional love. He will be a constant companion through good times and bad, playing with you or quietly curling up at your feet, always eager to please. This is why picking up a puppy for the first time and looking into those big brown eyes can very quickly make you throw all your reasoning out the window!

Before you fall completely under a puppy's spell, it is important to keep in mind that for the entire life of this dog, he will rely on you for everything, from the basic needs of food, water, shelter, and medical care, to physical needs, i.e., exercise, to his emotional needs, like mental stimulation and his education in the ways of the human world. Some people realize too late that a dog is a huge responsibility. If his needs are not met, a dog can grow to be anxious and unruly, if not outright destructive. That dream of a perfect pet can become a nightmare that you will be living in for the next 10 to 15 years. A dog is a long-term commitment and should not be treated like a piece of furniture that you can get rid of when you get tired of it.

With so much at stake, you should never get a dog on impulse. It is a serious endeavor that requires time and careful consideration, as well as the wisdom of those who have walked the trodden path.

REALITY CHECK

Are You Ready for a Dog?

Prior to getting a dog, it is essential that you do some real soul-searching. You need to be very clear about what you want to get out of this dog and how you picture him fitting into your current lifestyle. An eight-week-old puppy will demand a lot of your time and will very often seem like a 24-hour job. Toilet training alone requires constant supervision. He will also be looking to you for play and other stimulating activities several times a day. During this time you will be setting up his daily routine and teaching him how he is expected to behave in all human situations. Many have likened raising a dog to raising a child. They are right, except raising a dog may just be a bit harder.

Unlike the dogs that you see in the movies, real dogs have very real needs. Nutritious food and competent veterinary care to ensure their well-being are costs that can put a significant strain on your finances. And although you will be less likely to feel it, the bigger costs are the ones charged to your time. Here are some factors to consider before taking the plunge.

Time

If you have a nine-to-five job, you will find it very difficult to fit a dog into your schedule. It will be hard to fulfill your responsibilities without the help of co-parents (a *yaya*, a neighbor, or other family members). If he has to be left home alone the whole day, you set yourself up for some serious behavior issues, so it may be better not to get a dog. A dog is a social animal that does not thrive when left alone for long periods. It is a companion animal by nature and if you are away the whole day, you will have no choice but to rely on other people to look after his physical, social, and emotional needs, i.e., potty breaks, twice-a-day walks, training, exercise, play, and enriching experiences, throughout his life.

Space

The other consideration that new owners consciously or unconsciously overlook is the availability of space. At eight weeks old, a puppy will require only a small corner of the house dedicated to it. In no time, however, that cute little ball of fur will grow into a dog, and in the case of a large breed dog like a Labrador Retriever, will grow into a very big and energetic dog! And although small dogs will require a smaller space compared with big breeds, even they need enough space to move around freely.

If there are only two or three of you living in an apartment, having a small- to medium-sized dog is manageable. But if there are more people sharing that space and you plan on getting a big dog, then you may need to reconsider your plan.

Other People

Do the other people in your home like dogs? Are any of them allergic to dogs? Are they sensitive to the smell of a dog in the house? Are they willing to share parenthood and cooperate with you on the rules you set for raising your dog? These are very serious things to consider if you want your housemates to continue talking to you.

Once you've gone through this reality check and you are still positive about bringing a dog into your life, then go for it and don't look back. Find the right dog that will fit your lifestyle. The rewards you will reap are endless and you will soon realize that the love of a dog is truly priceless.

What Is the Right Dog for You?

Once you have made the decision to get a dog, choosing the RIGHT dog is now your primary concern. Here is a list of things to consider as you go about your search.

Purpose

For what purpose are you getting this dog? Is it for companionship or for competitions (either in conformation or in dog sports)? Dogs for companionship don't require much, as essentially any dog that is calm and enjoys the company of people will make a great companion. Conformation showing will, however, require a dog with special traits—a pure breed dog with the proper structure and looks to compete. It will also need to have the proper registration papers with the local canine club.

Dog sports, like agility or rally obedience, usually do not require registration papers but will require that your dog have the proper drives and temperament for such competitions. Dogs for more specific purposes such as Schutzhund (originally a dog sport used to test the breed suitability of German Shepherds; today it is used to measure the working ability of dogs) will require specific breeds as well as sound temperaments. These are high-performance dogs that will also demand stronger leadership and training skills from their owners.

Age

When most people acquire a dog, the usual choice would be a young puppy, which is probably best because a puppy is still very much like an empty hard drive. You still have the option to install the "programs" you want through early imprinting and training and you have greater flexibility to mold its behaviors to your preference.

Some people, however, prefer not to deal with the difficulties of raising a puppy, as many find it time-consuming to deal with things like potty training or laying down the foundation skills. Acquiring a young adult in this case is more preferable. But if you do choose to get a young adult dog, it is imperative that you acquire the dog from a breeder that you trust, one who has set the puppy with the proper habits and basic manners.

Gender

While the choice in gender may be considered a personal preference, significant differences between male and female dogs do exist. Male dogs tend to be bigger, more muscular, and typically more active than females. Hence, they demand more time for exercise than females. Males also have a higher tendency to mark, especially around other males, and can be expected to be more aggressive toward other dogs. Females, on the other hand, tend to demand—and give—more attention than males, making them the more preferred home companions. The downside, however, is that females will go into heat every six months and some people may find this inconvenient. Females in heat will menstruate for a week or so, leaving spots of blood as they move around the house. Plus, male dogs will go crazy around a female in heat so it can be difficult whenever she's around male dogs.

Breed

With over 600 breeds of dogs available today there can be too many breeds to make choosing an easy task. It's important that you remember that each pure breed dog was bred for a specific purpose. Herding, guarding, hunting—these jobs demand that the dog come with unique drives, looks, and abilities to do the job well.

Consider then that although a Golden Retriever makes a wonderful family dog, it will have the inherent traits of a hunting dog. It will love to chase small animals (like your pet cat!) and will have a consuming passion to tip over his water bowl and swim in the puddle he created. Jack Russell Terriers, while small and considered one of the most intelligent breeds, were also bred to be tenacious rat hunters and thus have a tendency to be scrappy dogs constantly looking for a good fight.

When choosing your preferred breed, it pays to read up on the history of that dog and the purpose for which its temperament was created. This way, his behavior will be more predictable and you will be able to choose a dog that will fit your particular lifestyle. If you are an active person who enjoys the outdoors, then you will probably do well with more active breeds with higher exercise requirements like hunting or herding dogs. If you are more of a sedentary person, then you will do better with a less energetic dog that is laid-back and prefers to curl up beside you on the couch. If you are very particular about cleanliness and order in your house and yard, then a less active, indoor-type breed is better for you as a high-energy outdoor dog like a Pointer or a Terrier will definitely have some ideas about redoing your interior decor and may install a pool in your yard, even if you didn't ask for one.

Other things to consider when choosing the breed of the dog you are getting are size, grooming requirements, and the presence of children in the household. The size of the breed you choose should be determined by how much space is available in your house. Condo dwellers will do better with smaller breeds as many buildings do not allow larger breeds. Larger, more active breeds are stronger dogs and will need physically stronger owners and access to a large exercise area like a yard or a nearby field. Size is also a consideration when there are children in the home. Small breeds like the Shih Tzu and Maltese are obvious choices, but "gentle giants" like the Newfoundland and the Bernese Mountain Dog are also great choices. Needless to say, kids and dogs must be closely supervised around each other at all times.

If you do not have much time and the patience to devote to grooming your dog on a daily basis then perhaps you would want to consider shorthaired breeds that don't have much combing and drying requirements. Longhaired breeds will require daily brushing and will pick up dirt very quickly when given access to the garden. Shedding is always an issue for most dogs and only a handful, like the Poodles and the Bichons, shed very little, but still require the same, if not a greater, amount of care for their coat.

Crosses and Mixes

You may also want to consider cross breeds or mixes. Cross breeds are dogs that are produced from crossing two different pure breed dogs. In most cases, these are accidents and the results can be appealing to some people. In fact, this has given rise to the popularity of what are now referred to as "designer dogs," with exotic names like Labradoodles or Cockapoos.

Mixed breeds are more randomly bred dogs, usually products of multiple crosses with hardly any human intervention. Being a mixed breed does not make a dog any less of a dog. They can be just as lovable and in many instances even healthier family companions than some pure breed dogs. Many mixes have gone on to become champions in dog sports like agility and frisbee competitions.

Being a mixed breed dog simply means that its traits are not as clear-cut as a pure breed and you may need to spend some time figuring out whether your mixed breed dog is more of a Terrier or a Poodle, a consideration that is important when you are dealing with his behavior during training. However, they do present a clear advantage over pure breed dogs. Because the pure breed dogs have developed from a small genetic base in order to produce consistency in shape, size, structure, and the overall general appearance, this has also concentrated undesirable genes that have increased medical risks. Heart disease in Cavalier Spaniels, skin issues in West Highland Terriers, hip and elbow dysplasia in German Shepherds are just some of the increased health risks in pure breeds. While mixes are prone to the same infections and injuries as pure breeds, they do enjoy a lower risk of inherited diseases.

A BASIC GUIDE TO

Dog Breeds

When choosing a dog breed that matches your lifestyle, it is important for you to know that most of these breeds were originally bred for a particular purpose. Each of these breeds has a unique set of traits and special needs that you have to consider should you decide to live with one.

Sporting Breeds

Sporting dogs were bred primarily to search and retrieve game birds and small mammals. These dogs are hardy, spirited dogs with a natural desire to please. Sociable, low in protection and territorial instincts, they make great family dogs when given enough exercise. They are generally easygoing and enjoy the companionship of their humans.

Great for young, active owners who love the outdoors, especially the water.

Sample Breeds: Labrador Retriever, Golden Retriever, Pointer, Cocker Spaniel, Irish Setter, Weimaraner

Herding Breeds

Hardworking, agile, and possessing high prey drives, herding dogs were bred for instinct and decision-making capabilities. These dogs are great problem solvers and can work independently without much supervision. Their protective instincts and independent

thinking also make them the best dogs for service duties such as police and military work, search and rescue, and assistance. Early socialization and training is a must to keep them from becoming overprotective.

Herding breeds need owners with great leadership skills and who can provide lots of exercise and mentally stimulating activities. These dogs do well in competitive sports like obedience, disc dog, agility, and Schutzhund.

Sample Breeds: German Shepherd, Belgian Malinois, Collie, Border Collie, Australian Shepherd, Shetland Sheepdog, Welsh Corgi

Working Breeds

Sturdy, strong, and ready to work when required, the dogs in the working group are as varied as the type of work they were bred to do—pull heavy loads, guard flock, patrol estates, aid fishermen, and rescue people. Many of these dogs have been working and assisting humans for hundreds of years, so they take their jobs seriously. Generally, these dogs are alert, courageous, hardy, protective, persistent, and dominant. They are great homebodies.

These guarding dogs, nordic dogs, and gentle giants will need owners that can provide alternative activities to the jobs they were bred to do. Although usually large and strong, they can also make great home companions.

Sample Breeds: St. Bernard, Newfoundland, Alaskan Malamute, Akita, Siberian Husky, Boxer, Bullmastiff, Doberman, Great Dane, Rottweiler, Samoyed, Standard Schnauzer

Hounds

If dogs have a great sense of smell, the dogs in this category have the best noses of them all. Traditionally used for tracking game, they come in two kinds: the *scent hounds* and the *sight hounds*. Scent hounds primarily use their noses and will relentlessly follow them to track rabbits, elk, and even mountain lions. Sight hounds are some of the fastest in the world of canines. They use their very sharp eyes to sight and chase small animals. Hounds are generally independent but get along well with other dogs as they were bred to hunt together in large groups. While scent hounds are generally prone to baying, sight hounds are more placid and aloof. Great for people who love the great outdoors, are runners or power walkers. They also make great detection dogs for military applications.

Sample Breeds: Bloodhound, Beagle, Dachshund, Basset Hound, Afghan Hound, Saluki, Greyhound, Whippet, Rhodesian Ridgeback

Terriers

Bred with high predatory instincts to hunt rodents underground, terriers are sturdy, fearless, highly energetic dogs built into a small package. Playful and feisty, they are admired for their spunk and resilience. They will not back down from a challenge

even when they face a much larger animal. Their fearless attitude makes them great watchdogs—and they bark a lot. So if you don't want a noisy dog, don't get a terrier!

Sample Breeds: Jack Russell Terrier, American Staffordshire Terrier, Bull Terrier, Miniature Schnauzer, West Highland Terrier, Scottish Terrier

Toys

From the Chinese Crested to the Pomeranian, the toy breeds were bred for companionship and entertainment. Many of them are scaled-down versions of larger breeds but do not necessarily have diminished drives. Some can be spunky while others are mild-mannered and sweet. Toy breeds do not demand much exercise, are inexpensive to feed, and require less effort to clean up. These are dogs that will live on your lap.

Sample Breeds: Cavalier King Charles Spaniel, Chihuahua, Maltese, Miniature Pinscher, Toy Poodle, Pekingese, Pomeranian, Chinese Crested, Shih Tzu, Pug, Yorkshire Terrier

Non-Sporting

Due to the wide diversity of dogs produced throughout history, there are dogs that are truly distinct individuals that do not share characteristics with dogs in the other categories. Hence, these are dogs classified as Non-Sporting breeds. Their purpose and their instincts vary greatly and will suit every taste.

Sample Breeds: Bichon Frise, English Bulldog, Boston Terrier, Chinese Sharpei, Chow Chow, Dalmatian, Shiba Inu, Lhasa Apso, Standard and Miniature Poodle

Where Puppies Are Available

In the Philippines, a discussion of this topic would probably fill up another book because of the wide variety of places you can get a puppy. Rather than ask where the best place to acquire a puppy is in the Philippines, ask where you have the best chances of getting a healthy puppy with good temperament, and the best answer is "wherever you will best be able to exercise your power of choice." Here then is a short, but by no means definitive, discussion of these places.

Animal Shelters

Before looking anywhere else, consider looking at your local animal shelters because there are so many dogs there looking for permanent homes. Adult dogs rescued from the streets or from abusive owners are always in need of new homes. The dogs are almost always mixed breeds and are either spayed or neutered to prevent further breeding. Some of them are pure breed dogs that have been abandoned or left behind during natural calamities and turn out to be very good companion dogs. Puppies are also available occasionally and adopted very quickly.

Dogs adopted from a shelter are often well-socialized and the staff exerts great effort in trying to match the right dogs to the adopters. Highly sociable and great with cats, many of these dogs will offer you the same love and affection as any pure breed dog. Shelters are a low-cost alternative source for pet dogs due in large part to the awareness campaigns of animal welfare groups.

Home and Hobby Breeders

Some of the healthiest puppies come from amateur breeders who breed by accident or intent. Usually conscientious and caring breeders, they do what they do for the love of the breed or their family pet, rather than for commercial gain. A few of the puppies from these breeders will be successful at conformation shows, but most will make great family pets.

Show Breeders

Generally regarded as the best source of high-quality puppies, show breeders normally have the breeding parents tested for hereditary diseases prior to breeding and will want to keep track of the puppies they produce. Some of them do not advertise and will only entertain inquiries from the referrals of their friends. Show breeders actively show their dogs in conformation shows to determine which puppies will be fit to breed as they continue to improve their stock. If they sell you a puppy, they will often require you to show it in conformation and get its championship title at the very least. However, there is no guarantee that the puppies will grow into show champions. It is not uncommon for puppies from these breeders to be priced as much as three to four times higher than those from other sources.

Commercial Breeders

Sadly, there exists a good number of breeders that breed purely for commercial gain and take advantage of the market demand for pure breed dogs. These breeders will normally have 200 to 300 dogs and puppies at a time and will very seldom provide the healthy and enriching environment required for puppies to thrive. For obvious reasons, the health and quality of the dogs are not carefully monitored.

Pet Shops

Probably the most popular places to acquire a puppy are pet shops. Centrally located and providing direct access to a wide variety of breeds of puppies, these shops offer a convenient option for many families with busy schedules. The wide selection of puppies on display that are immediately available account for the high turnover of puppies.

On the downside, it is also generally known that many puppies from some of these establishments are at risk of deadly diseases like parvovirus and distemper. More recently, many of these establishments have been vaccinating the puppies themselves instead of having them done by licensed veterinarians, further compromising the health of their puppies. As a result, it is not uncommon for puppies to die within several days after being brought home. If you get a puppy from these shops, be very conscious of its health and take it to a vet straightaway for a thorough health examination.

Choosing Your Puppy

No matter where you decide to get your new puppy, the choice you make when picking one from a litter will have the greatest bearing on your future relationship. So it helps when you are able to work things in your favor. If possible, choose from the entire litter rather than from the last one or two that were left behind. It also helps to choose when the puppy is around seven weeks old, by which time his motor and sensory skills have developed and he is beginning to explore the world outside of his litter. This is also a period when the puppies' behavior have had little influence from their environment. Ask to see the mom and dad of the litter as they will be good indicators of what the puppies will grow into. Be wary when the breeder refuses to let you see either parent even if they are onsite. Great breeders will proudly show off the dam and sire.

When choosing a puppy from a litter, keep in mind that even though all of the puppies are of the same breed, they will each have their unique temperament. Some may be more fearful and submissive, while others will be brimming with confidence and are more socially dominant. Some will be more energetic while others may be more laid-back. In order to choose wisely, one must be able to distinguish clearly between the individual temperaments.

Remember, you want to choose a puppy that is right for you, so be careful not to get carried away by wagging tails and eager face licks. Their small sizes make them deceivingly easy to handle that you may overlook the fact that these puppies will eventually grow into bigger and stronger dogs that bear all the general characteristics of their breed.

How well you can predict the temperament of the *adult* dog that it will grow into and how well you choose the puppy that will most likely fit your personality and lifestyle will have great bearing on the success of your relationship with your dog. Great breeders have long recognized this and have traditionally relied on their experience and observations to try and figure out which puppy would best be suited to a prospective buyer's personality and lifestyle. Today, through the scientific efforts of people like Scott and Fuller, Clarence Pffafenberger, William Campbell, and Jack and Wendy Volhard, there exists a more reliable series of temperament tests that can predict, to a certain degree, what personality a puppy will grow into so that pairings between puppies and owners are more successful. Many variations have been made to these tests and every breeder or trainer would most likely have his own modified version.

Here is a typical puppy temperament test. It can help give a quick indication of the puppy's natural attitude toward people and a relative measure of his sociability. Note that it is not a fool-proof predictor of the puppy's adult personality as environment will also greatly influence that. It is, at most, a guide to help you figure out what type of home and what kind of training will work to bring out the best in the puppy.

The Puppy Temperament Test

GUIDELINES

- The test is done at seven weeks or the 49th day of the puppy's life.
- Each puppy is tested individually at the same activity level.
- The test must be done in a totally new environment, away from the noise of the litter, and with as few distractions as possible.
- It must be done at a time of the day when the puppies are normally active or playing.
- The tester must be a person unknown to the puppies.
- Each puppy must be given some time to potty before the test.
- The tests are done in the sequence listed.

PUPPY ID ____________ LITTER ____________ AGE OF LITTER ____________

TESTER ____________ DATE ____________

NOTETAKER ____________

TEST		SCORE	
RECOVERY The puppy is placed in a room that he hasn't been in and where the floor is lined with an assortment of surface materials, i.e., cardboard, a piece of carpet, a sheet of bubble wrap, etc. He is placed on one of the surfaces and his behavior is observed.	**Measures degree of confidence or fearfulness and ability to recover from a stressful situation**	Starts running around right away, investigating the environment	1
		Stands in place, looks around, then investigates	2
		Stands in place, looks around, then investigates, whines	3
		Runs around underfoot and whines	4
		Stands in place and doesn't move	5
		Runs away and hides	6
PLAY DRIVE Using a soft rope or plush toy attached to the end of a light leash, the tester presents the toy on the floor and uses the leash to move it around, encouraging the puppy to play.	**Measures degree of desire and willingness to engage in play, confidence**	Looks, chases, bites, and holds toy	1
		Looks, chases, doesn't grab the toy	2
		Looks, attempts to investigate	3
		Looks, barks, tucks tail in	4
		Ignores the toy	5
		Runs away	6

TEST		SCORE	
SOCIAL ATTRACTION The tester kneels on the floor a few feet away from the puppy and coaxes it to come by clapping his hands gently or calling, "Puppy! Puppy!"	**Measures degree of social attraction, confidence, or dependence**	**Comes readily, tail up, jumps, barks, mouths on tester's hands**	**1**
		Comes readily, tail up, paws and/or licks tester's hands	**2**
		Comes readily, tail up	**3**
		Comes readily, tail down	**4**
		Comes hesitantly or doesn't come, fearful	**5**
		Does not come at all, wanders and sniffs	**6**
FOLLOWING From the previous test, the tester stands up and walks away from the puppy, making sure the pup sees him walk away.	**Measures the desire to follow. Not following is an indication of independence or fear.**	**Follows readily, tail up, stays close, bites at tester's feet**	**1**
		Follows readily, tail up, stays close	**2**
		Follows readily, tail up	**3**
		Follows readily, tail down	**4**
		Huddles, doesn't move	**5**
		Doesn't follow or goes away	**6**
RESTRAINT Tester gets on the floor with the puppy and gently rolls him over on his back, and holds him with one hand for 30 seconds.	**Measures dominance/ submissive tendency and how it accepts stress when socially/physically dominated**	**Struggles fiercely, flails, bites**	**1**
		Vigorously flails, some eye contact	**2**
		Settles, struggles a bit, settles with good eye contact	**3**
		Struggles, then settles with some eye contact	**4**
		No struggle—freezes	**5**
		No struggle, strains to avoid eye contact	**6**
RETRIEVING Tester kneels by pup and attracts his attention with crumpled paper. When pup shows interest, tester tosses the object three feet in front of the pup.	**Measures degree of willingness to work with a human. High correlation between ability to retrieve and successful guide dogs, obedience dogs, field trial dogs.**	**Chases object, picks it up, and runs away**	**1**
		Chases object, picks it up, and doesn't return it	**2**
		Chases object, returns with it to tester	**3**
		Chases object and returns to tester without it	**4**
		Stays with tester, worried	**5**
		Doesn't chase the object	**6**

TEST		SCORE	
SOUND SENSITIVITY Tester places pup in the center of area, strikes pan with a large spoon a few feet behind the puppy. Repeats.	**Measures degree of sensitivity to sound. May be a rudimentary test for deafness.**	**Listens, locates sound, walks toward it barking**	**1**
		Listens, locates sound, shows curiosity, walks toward it	**2**
		Listens, orients toward sound	**3**
		Listens, startled	**4**
		Cringes, backs off, hides	**5**
		Ignores sound, shows no curiosity	**6**
SIGHT SENSITIVITY Tester places pup in the center of area, jerks a towel tied to a string across the floor a few feet from the puppy.	**Measures degree of intelligent response to a strange object**	**Looks, attacks, bites**	**1**
		Looks, grabs item, head shaking	**2**
		Looks, becomes curious	**3**
		Looks, tail tucked	**4**
		Runs away, hides	**5**
		Ignores it, shows no interest	**6**
ENERGY LEVEL Note how active pup is throughout the testing.	▪ **Constantly jumping** ▪ **Frisky** ▪ **Alert but relaxed**	▪ **Slow, quiet** ▪ **Little participation** ▪ **No interest**	

ANALYSIS OF PUPPY TEST

Mostly 1 and 2 responses

This is going to be a very strong, highly active dog that can be difficult to control. It will need firm and consistent training and it would be best go to an experienced trainer. This dog will need a full-time job. This is not a dog to take home as a pet.

Mostly 2 and 3 responses

The dog is enthusiastic and eager to please but needs a firm hand and lots of physical and mental stimulation or it will be difficult to live with. Obedience training is a must.

Mostly 3 responses, with some 4s

This will be a happy dog and it will be good with children. This dog will be good enough even for an inexperienced trainer and would make a great family companion.

Mostly 4 responses

This is a submissive but not shy puppy. You will need to help build its confidence. It is trainable and gets along with everybody.

Mostly 5 responses

This is a very shy puppy that needs to go to a low-stress environment. Only positive-reinforcement training is allowed—and it will need a lot of socialization.

Mostly 6 responses

This is a highly independent and/or shy puppy. This dog doesn't require a lot of human attention. Training requires a lot of motivation and patience. It will not make a good family pet.

Bringing Your Puppy Home

Now that you have chosen the puppy that is just right for you, we come to the exciting part where you take him home. Not too many things compare to the excitement of making preparations for the new addition to the family. At the same time, it can also cause anxiety over trying to get things right. So you can expect that the first few days with the puppy can be trying as both of you adjust to each other: you with having to adjust your lifestyle to fit in the new puppy, and the puppy having to deal with a completely new environment without his dam and littermates. With a bit of understanding, patience, and a sense of humor, you can make it a positive experience for both of you.

When raising a dog, the key to success is preparation and staying ahead of any eventuality. Before the puppy's arrival, there are things that you will need to plan ahead of time and equipment you will want to have on hand. These include:

- Having a supply of food (initially the same brand the breeder has been feeding him) as well as having separate food and water bowls
- Identifying an appropriate potty area
- Figuring out where the puppy will be staying when you are out of the house
- Figuring out where the puppy will be sleeping and providing a comfortable bed or crate for him to sleep in
- Having a set of toys appropriate for the age of your puppy

These are important things you don't want to have to think of when he is already running around your living room.

Food and Water

Starting with the basic needs, you will want to ask the breeder what food your puppy has been eating and have some of it in stock. Feeding the puppy a different brand can cause diarrhea so it's important to feed him the same food before deciding to switch to your preferred brand. If you think that the breeder's food is of poor quality, your pet professional should be able to give you sound advice on what brands are more beneficial for your puppy. Water must also be available to your puppy at all times. With young puppies, it is best to give cool, clean, and fresh water. If you are unsure of the quality of the water from the faucet, then it is better to give your pup bottled water. Puppies and dogs

get diarrhea from time to time and you want to be able to rule out his food and water as the cause. Remember that you should only give your dog water that you will drink yourself.

Puppy Playpen or Baby Gates

One of the most useful tools you can invest in is a folding puppy playpen. This is a very versatile tool initially used to keep your puppy confined to a small area or a corner of the house while his toilet training is not yet complete. Later on, it can serve to block off areas that are off-limits to your puppy, like the space under the computer table with all the electrical wires or the area around the trash can in the kitchen. You can also use baby gates to close off access to rooms where you don't want the puppy going into. If you are unable to find puppy fencing or baby gates, a large corrugated board with a chair behind it makes a good substitute.

Crate or Kennel

A plastic crate or kennel is also useful to have around as it provides a safe and comfortable place for your puppy to run to if he wants some quiet alone time. A crate is also used when traveling with the dog in the car as it keeps him relaxed and out of your way during car rides. The crate must never be used as a cage or as punishment and will thus require some basic training so the dog never feels he is forced to stay inside.

Bed or Cushion

Your puppy will appreciate having a soft bed or cushion to lie on, sleep on, or just hang out in, especially if he stays in an airconditioned room. Beds can also be useful tools for training as you can teach him to stay on his bed instead of pestering your guests when they come visit (this is part of basic manners when you enroll in obedience classes). Teaching your dog to stay on his bed is better than keeping him confined in another room or in a cage during times of social activity. Note that some dogs, especially northern breeds like Siberian Huskies, Chow Chows, and even Labrador Retrievers, prefer to lie on cold kitchen tiles. Even then, teaching them to stay on a bed will be another way to keep your dog under control.

Toys

One of the best ways to ease a dog into a new environment or situation is through play. Play is made much more interesting when toys are involved, so get your dog a variety of toys to stimulate him physically and mentally. Some of the most interesting toys are stuffed toys with squeakers inside. Balls are also great exercise toys as dogs will love to chase and retrieve them. Remember to choose a ball that is small enough for your puppy to carry in his mouth, but not too small that he might swallow it. Tug toys like ropes or balls on a rope are great toys to use when interacting with your dog. Chews, particularly the soft and edible ones made of cornstarch, are great for keeping the puppy busy and away from your expensive Pradas. Avoid rawhides, please.

Puppy Proofing Your Home

You will save yourself a lot of stress if you puppy-proof your house before the puppy comes home. Since you will be introducing him to the different parts of the house, you won't want him getting into certain things that should be off-limits. The best way to start this is to look at everything at knee-level and below and identify the things you will need to keep out of your puppy's reach. These include electrical and telephone cords, phone chargers, and drapes and table cloths that your puppy will pull on. Look at your shelves and elevate all items that you don't want chewed up or broken.

You may also need to close off certain areas of the house, like rooms with expensive Persian carpets or antique furniture. Stairs, balconies, and swimming pools also present serious risks to a puppy so you will need to close off access to these areas of the house. Needless to say, close off areas where the puppy may have access to toxic items like household cleaners, medication, anti-freeze, poisonous plants, and garbage.

The Age of the Puppy

Most breeders agree that the best time to release a puppy from its litter is between the ages of seven and 10 weeks. This is when the puppy has been fully weaned from its dam and has been eating solid puppy food for some time. It is also within the period of socialization when the puppy is just beginning to explore the world outside of his litter and is starting to form relationships with people, places, and other dogs. This is the best time to bring home a puppy so he can form bonds with the people in your family as well as other pets. If you take a puppy away from his litter too soon, he will miss out on some very important social lessons that he needs to learn from his dam and littermates, which can cause some serious behavior issues later on. If you take him home after the socialization window has closed at 16 weeks, you will miss out on the golden opportunity to bond closely with him and ease him through all sorts of novel and potentially traumatic experiences.

The Car Ride Home

When picking up the puppy, it is always best to have someone with you, to assist you in handling him especially if you have to drive. It is best to hold the puppy and keep him on your or your companion's lap so there's a reassuring presence as he goes on makes this first car ride. Many dogs grow up barking incessantly or salivating excessively during car rides. Very often, the reason is that the dog's first experience riding in a car was an adverse one, imprinted on the dog's psyche for the rest of his life.

For safety reasons, the puppy should be carried by another person in the back seat if you are driving the car yourself. Putting him in the front opens up the possibility of the puppy crawling onto your lap while you're driving or ending up at your feet beneath the pedals. It is best if someone keeps him company in the back seat, talking to him and distracting him with a favorite toy from his former home. This is much better than placing him alone in a box as he is being taken away from his birth family for the first and possibly the last time. Try to make the car ride as smooth and relaxed for the puppy as possible. Avoid going over rough roads and take it easy on the brakes. The more pleasant you make this first car ride, the more enjoyable his future car rides are going to be.

Arrival

Upon arriving at home, you would have instructed everyone not to fuss too much over the new puppy so as not to overwhelm him. Keep things upbeat but low-key. Keep the kids quiet and teach them to be calm and gentle around the puppy.

The first thing the puppy is going to want to do when he arrives is to potty. The anxiety of being thrust into this new and unfamiliar environment with all sorts of new people will make any dog want to relieve himself. So take him immediately to the place you've identified as his potty area and allow him to sniff around for a bit. If you've brought home a very young puppy and his vaccinations are not yet complete, do not take him into the garden just yet, as he will still be at risk of getting a fatal infection. Let him go instead on an indoor potty pad or a tray with an old carpet that you've prepared beforehand (see Toilet Training). If the breeder has gotten the puppy used to going on newspapers, then having some newspaper on the floor might be a better option. If the puppy potties successfully in the designated area, make sure you reward him because this first experience will set the tone for the rest of his toilet training.

One of the biggest mistakes people make when they bring home a puppy is to give him free run of the house. This is when the puppy gets into all sorts of trouble, chewing on things and peeing or pooping all over the house. Avoid this by keeping him confined in a small part of the house in the beginning, allowing him to sniff around and get used to that area only. There will be plenty of time in the coming days and weeks to introduce him to the other parts of the house, so there's no need to rush. Keep the puppy with you at all times, closing off access to other parts of the house so you can always keep an eye on him. Get him to relax by offering him some food or water or maybe even having the other members of the household call him and offer him treats or play. This will make him form positive associations with the new people he meets in the house. Give him one or two of the toys you bought previously and see which ones will excite him, and play with him a bit. Food and toys are always great stress relievers! It is important that someone stays with the puppy during the first few hours in his new home. If you must leave him, leave him with someone just so that he doesn't feel alone while he is still familiarizing himself with his new home. If you need to do some work and cannot supervise him, confine him in the puppy playpen, but only after he's been pottied and exercised.

Toilet Training

To a new pet owner, the most vexing part of raising a puppy is probably toilet training. This begins the moment you take the puppy home. Many times, new owners get so caught up in the moment that they forget that the most pressing need of the puppy when he arrives is to relieve himself. Anxious about the new environment and not knowing where the toilet is, the poor puppy is forced to relieve himself where he is—indoors, catching everyone completely unaware. Everyone then screams in panic, scaring the already anxious puppy as though he'd done something so horrible. From then on, the puppy learns that he shouldn't potty in the presence of his humans because they get mad when he does. What's worse, some humans will even drag the young puppy and shove his little nose in his poop. That poor puppy will now look for some hidden corner to do his business, or will wait until the humans are out of sight before doing it.

If you are fortunate enough to have acquired your puppy from a great breeder, he would have already started the puppy with paper training. This teaches the puppy to do his business in one place consistently instead of doing it everywhere. So when you get home, the only thing you will have to remember is to have some newspaper lying around near the puppy all the time. Otherwise, you will need to start the training from scratch.

The truth is that dogs by nature will not want to soil the areas where they sleep or lie on. They will actually prefer to do it outside, their default potty area. However, because we keep them confined indoors with no access to the outdoors, they don't have much of a choice but to do it in the places that approximate that default potty area. These are the areas that smell like soil and feel like grass—the carpet or doormats! In fact, he will pretty much see anything that smells like soil as a potential potty area, which is practically anywhere in the house where we walk with our shoes on!

Once a dog has peed or pooped in a particular spot in the house, the scent

"Young puppies don't have full control of their bladders yet, so you need to accept that accidents will happen."

Toilet Training

of the urine or feces will remain there for a while even after you've cleaned it up. This is why the dog keeps going back to the same place and doing it there. So the first step in toilet training is to clean up all the spots in the house that the dog has soiled. You need to use an enzyme cleaner like Nature's Miracle which many people swear by. After cleaning up the mess, spray it with Nature's Miracle and leave it for about 15 minutes. Then clean it up again. For porous surfaces like wood, you may need to do this several times before the scent disappears. If Nature's Miracle is not available, a good substitute is a 20 percent vinegar solution. That's one part vinegar, four parts water. It doesn't smell as nice as Nature's Miracle but it's cheap, readily available, and it works. Do not use ammonia-based cleaners as these tend to enhance the scent of urine rather than eliminate it.

After cleaning up the soiled areas, you don't want your puppy soiling any part of the house again, so keep him confined to a small area until he has become reliable with his toilet habits. Young puppies don't have full control of their bladders yet so you need to accept that one of the realities of toilet training is that ACCIDENTS WILL HAPPEN. Confining the pup in a small area limits the accidents to only that area, and a puppy playpen can help you with this.

The Potty Area

The next thing you need to do is to choose a spot with a particular surface that you want your puppy to recognize as a potty area. As mentioned earlier, dogs and puppies are very aware of the surface that they potty on and that the default surface is grass. You can, however, teach him to go reliably on others surfaces like concrete, tile, or whatever you think is most practical for your situation. What's important is that once you've chosen the surface and the location, you must always consistently bring your puppy there to potty.

One of the difficulties of potty training puppies is that until their vaccinations are complete, you cannot bring them outside without the risk of getting a deadly infection. Also, if you live on the 25th floor of a condominium, the garden is not

Toilet Training

easily accessible. The solution to this is to make a small indoor potty place, similar to a cat litter box, where the puppy can potty. You can use a large plastic tray or the rubber trays that you put in the trunk of the car. It needs to be large enough to accommodate your puppy so that he can turn around with a bit of freedom. Fill the tray with sod—the square of grass that you can get from gardening stores. Dirt, sand, or even concrete are other alternatives if your dog or puppy is going to go on these surfaces later on. Some people don't find dirt acceptable inside the house, so you can try using a piece of old carpeting or cheap, scrap fabric doormats you can get at the supermarket. The advantage of using these is that you can use them to wipe off accidents, automatically putting the scent of the puppy's own urine on it. This helps him identify the mat as his potty place. The downside is that the dog learns to potty on carpets and doormats. Newspaper and pee pads are not generally recommended as they can create confusion when you transition the dog to going outside. Plus, some dogs will make the pad a play thing and shred it to pieces.

Once you've built your indoor potty tray, you can enclose this in a small puppy play fence so that when you place the puppy in it, he won't be able to do his business anywhere else except on the potty tray. Place the tray in a quiet area of the house, away from his sleeping area as well as from things that may distract him from pottying.

Knowing Your Puppy's Potty Schedule

Aside from a consistent potty surface, another key point of potty training is knowing when your puppy needs to go. When you know that it's about that time, you can bring your puppy there even before he thinks he has to go. Consider that if you feed your puppy three times a day, then you can also expect him to poop three times a day. Peeing is a little more difficult to predict as the puppy is constantly drinking throughout the day. But generally, a new puppy will pee every 30 minutes. That means he needs to be taken to the potty area every 30 minutes. As he gets older, the 30-minute cycle changes and becomes longer and longer.

Toilet Training

There are predictable times when your puppy will very likely have to go and it is important to be aware of them at all times:

- After waking up in the morning or after a nap
- After eating or drinking
- After or in the middle of playing and running around
- Before and after car rides
- When arriving at a new place
- When meeting a new person or another dog

Taking your puppy regularly to the potty place every 30 minutes or so and taking him during these predictable times will increase your chances of getting the puppy to go in the right place. Give him enough time to do his business, maybe around five to 10 minutes. And when your puppy gets it right, make sure you reward him immediately after he does the deed. Rewarding the puppy with a treat every time he gets it right also increases the likelihood that your dog will choose to potty in the right place.

As your dog matures, you will need to take him for potty breaks every three hours or so. By this time, he should have more control of his bladder and bowel movement that he can hold it for longer periods. For now, it is important to give him as many opportunities as possible to go to his potty area.

Recognizing the Signs

Just before a puppy has to pee or poop, he will exhibit signs that you should be able to recognize instantly. One of the first signs is when he starts to lose focus on what he is doing. For example if he is playing and suddenly stops in the middle to sniff around, you should check to see if your puppy is about to go. If he starts to sniff around in circles, this is a good indicator that he REALLY has to go. This is the time to pick him up and bring him to the potty area.

Teaching Him to Potty On Command

When you catch your puppy at the right time and bring him to the potty area, be like a tree and try not to get him excited or he may want to play instead of potty. Start chanting your potty command as he sniffs around. "Go potty" or "hurry up" are some common commands you can use. Keep saying this until he lowers his behind to finally do his business. As soon as he finishes, praise your dog and reward him with his favorite

Toilet Training

treat. Then take him out of the potty place. The more successful you are at pottying your dog in the potty place, the more the puppy will associate the potty command with the act of pottying.

When Accidents Occur

It is only reasonable to expect accidents to happen as you are just starting your puppy's potty training so do not stress over it too much. Otherwise, your puppy will sense your anxiety and may become anxious himself. There will be times when your attention will be diverted and you may miss the signs. If you are too late and you catch your puppy already squatting and doing it, forget about trying to bring him to the potty area. You will only either interrupt what he has started or make an even bigger mess than if you had just let him finish. Do not panic and make a big fuss either so as not to frighten the puppy. Just bite your lip and quietly go find something with which you can clean up the mess. Do better next time.

If you bring your puppy to the potty area and he doesn't go, maybe he just doesn't feel like going at that time. If he really has to go, he will probably go within a few minutes. If not, take him back to his playpen, but keep an eye on him just in case. You could also try to stimulate his urge to go by playing with him and making him run around. Then bring him to the potty area and try again.

The Importance of Supervision

Supervising your puppy while he is pottying is just as important as both taking him consistently to the same potty area and taking him there at the right time. Many people will send their dogs out into the garden to potty and then go back to cooking or working inside the house. Unknown to them, all the dog did was to run around and play the whole time he was outside. So when the owner finally lets him in the house, the puppy realizes that he forgot to do his business and ends up doing it inside! Supervision ensures that you are able to note when your puppy last went and you are able to reward your puppy for pottying in the right place. More importantly, you are able to teach your dog a potty command so that when you go out to other homes or establishments, you will be able to ask your dog to potty outside before going in and prevent an unwelcome incident.

Introducing The Crate

The crate or kennel is one of the best things you can get for your dog. Oftentimes people do get them but end up using them for the wrong reasons, like caging or for punishment. The main use of a crate is for traveling with your dog, either in a car or when flying in a plane. Either way, your dog will have to stay in the crate, confined for long periods. So it only makes sense that you teach your dog how to stay in a crate and LOVE staying in a crate for long periods. Considering their lupine heritage, dogs naturally love sleeping in dens or small dark spaces in the ground. For them, a den provides safety from both the elements and potential predators. A crate offers the same benefits and makes perfect sense as a bedroom for your dog.

For a crate to be effective, it must be big enough for your dog to stand and sit in without hitting his head on the roof of the crate. It should also be wide enough for him to be able to turn around and lie down. The plastic ones with a wire mesh gate are preferred. However, if you already have a wire crate, you can place a large cloth over and around it so it keeps things dark and covered.

When you introduce the crate, the puppy or dog may be apprehensive of it at first; this is normal. Help him get over his apprehension by throwing high-value treats or his favorite toys inside and allow him to go in and get it. Keep the door open and let him do this in his own time. Once he is going in on his own, start feeding him all his meals inside the crate so that he makes positive associations with it. You can also tie a chew

toy or peanut butter-filled Kong toy to the back of the crate to encourage him to spend longer periods inside the crate.

As he gets used to spending time in the crate, you can start closing its door. Initially, keep the door closed for one minute. Work gradually until you can keep it closed for 30 minutes to an hour. Remember that before you get your dog in the crate he must already be tired from play and exercise and pottied so that all he has to do inside is sleep. Do not keep your dog locked in the crate to a point where he will be barking and scratching at the door to get out. He must never feel like he was trapped in there or he will never want to go back in. As a rule of thumb, older dogs should not be kept in a crate for longer than three to four hours at a time. Keeping the dog in a crate overnight is okay as their systems slow down when they're asleep.

The First Night

On the puppy's first night home, he can become anxious and fearful when he is suddenly left alone. He may start to look for the familiar presence of his dam and littermates. To help ease him through this period, it is best to have him spend the night with you in your bedroom. It is not necessary to have him on your bed, just have him sleep on the floor beside you, enclosed in a play pen so that he doesn't go wandering around during the night. You can place his crate in the potty area, keeping the door open and his preferred toys inside the crate. You may want to include a stuffed toy or a pillow in case he looks for something to snuggle up to during the night. You can also place the potty tray in the pen with him as he may need to go during the night. Otherwise he may wake you up with his whining and you will have to get up and take him out to potty.

Usually by nighttime, a puppy will be exhausted and will sleep through the night. Some will wake up to potty but will be able to go back to sleep. Others may try to get you to play. Try not to give in to this or you will be spending a lot of sleepless nights. It helps to turn off the lights at bedtime as a cue that it is time to sleep.

Letting the puppy sleep in your bedroom should only be temporary if you plan to move him out later on. If you do, then you should only allow this for no longer than the first three nights at home. Beyond that, the puppy may find it difficult to sleep away from you, so you should probably decide on this by the first night.

Building a Routine

Dogs are more relaxed when they are able to predict what will happen throughout the day, so one of the best things you can do for your dog is to put him on a daily routine and follow it consistently. A normal dog's day isn't really much more than wake up, potty, hunt (exercise), eat, potty, play, sleep—repeated three times a day. After meeting his basic needs of pottying and eating, a dog needs physical and mental stimulation so that he will be tired enough to sleep. Once these needs are met, a dog will sleep, and they will sleep for long hours at a time in the safety of the home. Who could ask for a better life?

CHAPTER 2

Understanding Your Dog's Club Certificate

Here in the Philippines, there is a number of different clubs for dogs. Many of them are breed-specific, such as the Shih Tzu Fanciers Club of the Philippines and the Miniature Schnauzer Club of the Philippines, Inc., while others include entire breed groups. The Philippine Canine Club, Inc. (PCCI) and the Asian Kennel Club Union of the Philippines, Inc. (AKCUPI) are the organizations that mainly deal with registering pure breed dogs in the country.

Once you register your pup, he will be given a certificate. The certificate shows that your new dog is yours and provides extensive details on your dog's lineage, going beyond his mom and dad (or dam and sire, respectively), back to his ancestors. Take a look at your dog's certificate and you can see where he inherited his color and markings, and also find out if he hails from a family of champions. (Of course, you won't love him any less if he doesn't have any champion ancestors!)

A lot of breeders and owners put a premium on pure breed dogs "with papers." If you have a pure breed dog, chances are he will have papers or a certificate from either of the two local dog clubs: PCCI or AKCUPI.

Here's a useful reminder: Always make sure your pure breed dog has all his papers. If you have just gotten a pure breed dog, but he doesn't have any papers, then he won't be qualified to register for any of these clubs.

Apart from providing registration services for pure breed dogs and their owners, both PCCI and AKCUPI work to promote the canine industry and proper pet ownership. Dog shows and other events are held regularly by both organizations. Even if you're not planning to enter your dog in competitions, they give you a great opportunity to mingle with other dog owners and enthusiasts—and even check out their adorable pets and help your own dog make new friends.

Registering with PCCI

Established in 1963, PCCI is affiliated with the American Kennel Club, the Canadian Kennel Club, and The Kennel Club of UK. PCCI also registers dogs imported from other countries.

If you're getting your puppy from a breeder, you don't need to worry about registering your puppy. A transfer of ownership is all you need here, since your puppy, along with his littermates, has already been registered with PCCI. You want to make sure that the puppy has a Certified Registration and Pedigree Certificate so ownership can be transferred to you. To do this, you need to first become a member of PCCI. Download the PCCI Membership Card form from www.pcci.org.ph, or fill one out at their office. You need to include two ID photos and prepare P540, which will pay for your membership fee, admission fee, and ID card. Then submit all the documents at the PCCI office.

Member of: Federation Cynologique Internationale (F.C.I.)
Asia Kennel Union (A.K.U.)
Reciprocal Agreement with:
American Kennel Club (AKC)
Canadian Kennel Club (CKC)
The Kennel Club, U.K. (KC)

PCCI

PHILIPPINE CANINE CLUB, INC.

CERTIFIED PEDIGREE & REGISTRATION CERTIFICATE

№ 586735

Name of Dog: SOUTHSKY'S DAY TO REMEMBER
Breed: PUG
Sex: MALE
Date of Birth: October 01, 2011
Breeder: MR. JON JEFFREY M YAMAS
Transfer: N/A
Color: FAWN BLACK MASK
Owner: MR. JON JEFFREY M YAMAS
Address: # 23 SAN ISIDRO ST SKYLINE VILL CATALUNAN GRANDE DAVAO CITY
PCCI Reg. No.: 32288N5
Foreign Reg. No.:
Microchip No.:
Tattoo No.:
Litter No.: 65693T 111001 2,0

Sire 1 PHIL CH DOS AMIGOS CREAM OF D CROP 28362N5 FAWN BLACK MASK
Dam 2 UNCLE MARC'S RAGING GEM 26115N5 FAWN BLACK MASK

3 PHIL GR CH TROJAN PUG FORTUNE HUNTER 9836N5 FAWN BLACK MASK
4 PHIL GR CH TROJAN PUG KISS ME KATE 19631N5 FAWN BLACK MASK
5 PHIL HOF TROJAN PUG LUCKY STRIKE 9588N5 FAWN
6 SILVERSTAR AM A CUTIE 12234N5 FAWN BLACK MASK

7 PHIL / CAN CH JIMARY'S MOONLIGHT GAMBLER (CAN) 4253N5 CKC LL738493 FAWN
8 PHIL CH FORBEST BRADY LI'L RASCAL 5355N5 FAWN BLACK MASK
9 PHIL CH TROJAN PUG MY MASTERPIECE 15765N5 FAWN BLACK MASK
10 PHIL CH TROJAN PUG CHRYSELL REINE 4631N5 FAWN BLACK MASK (GR DAM OF MERIT)
11 PHIL HOF FORBEST BLACK MOON RISING 5295N5 FAWN BLACK MASK (GR SIRE OF MERIT)
12 BUSHADDAM OMAR SHAH 4177N5 FAWN BLACK MASK
13 PHIL CH FORBEST FINAL FLAME 7091N5 FAWN
14 PHIL CH ANNIE OF LULUBELLE'S COTY 6424N5 FAWN BLACK MASK

15 CAN CH JIMARY'S JUST TOMMY CKC HY564696
16 CAN CH JIMARY'S EMMA BABY SPICE CKC HN519445
17 PHIL HOF/AM CH SIMON SHENGCHEE DANCING TIGER (USA) 4607N5 AKC TP227020/01 FAWN (SIRE OF MERIT)
18 YANG'S LION BEAR QUEEN 4324N5 FAWN BLACK MASK
19 PHIL HOF FORBEST BLACK MOON RISING 5295N5 FAWN BLACK MASK (GR SIRE OF MERIT)
20 COCOY'S FLORE 10027N5 FAWN BLACK MASK (DAM OF MERIT)
21 LIVEDRUM'S DIAMOND 4321N5 FAWN BLACK MASK
22 HURRICANE ICE BATHSHEBA 3192N5 FAWN BLACK MASK
23 PHIL HOF/AM CH SIMON SHENGCHEE DANCING TIGER (USA) 4607N5 AKC TP227020/01 FAWN (SIRE OF MERIT)
24 HEAVEN'S PLACE BELLE O' LUV 3403N5 FAWN BLACK MASK
25 PHIL CH SIDNEY'S ONE ON ONE 2048N5 FAWN BLACK MASK
26 BUSHADDAM MAGIC WAND 1558N5 FAWN BLACK MASK
27 PHIL HOF/AM CH SIMON SHENGCHEE DANCING TIGER (USA) 4607N5 AKC TP227020/01 FAWN (SIRE OF MERIT)
28 SAMBALI'S JOLLY HEATHER 4809N5 FAWN BLACK MASK
29 PHIL CH COTY'S SPUNKY INTIMIDATOR 1568N5 FAWN
30 PHIL HOF TINKERBELL OF NOSWAH'S ARK 3548N5 FAWN BLACK MASK

SAMPLE ONLY

PHILIPPINE CANINE CLUB INCORPORATED PCCI 1963

Date Issued January 27, 2012

I certify that these Pedigree & Registration Certificates were obtained from the official Stud Books of the Philippine Canine Club, Inc.

Authorized Signature

Once you're a member, you can begin processing the transfer of ownership. Fill out the transfer ownership information at the back of the Pedigree Certificate. The original owner or breeder will write down the date when you acquired the dog and your name and address. Both of you have to sign the back of the certificate. Remember that the dog can only be registered once with a registering body.

Registering with AKCUPI

AKCUPI was established in 2008 and is affiliated with the following groups: Federacion Canina Internacional based in Valencia, Spain, the International Kennel Union based in Russia, the Union of Asian Kennel Clubs based in Korea, and the Kennel Club Union of Asia based in Taiwan.

Registering with AKCUPI is a fairly simple process. You can get an application form at their office in Quezon City or on their website, www.akcupi.com. Bring your dog's original pedigree certificate to their office; AKCUPI also accepts PCCI-registered dogs. You also need to provide them with your information. If you're a new registrant, you have to submit an ID photo which will be used for your own dog owner's ID. If you're registering a litter, keep in mind that both parents should be registered with AKCUPI. The litter registration form should be signed by the owners of the dam and sire.

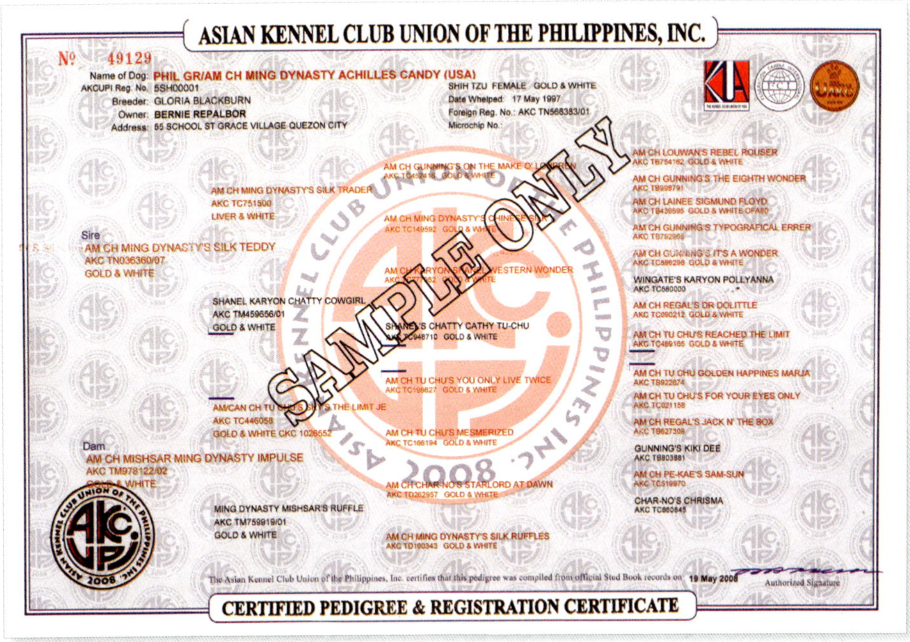
ASIAN KENNEL CLUB UNION OF THE PHILIPPINES, INC.

№ 49129

Name of Dog: PHIL GR/AM CH MING DYNASTY ACHILLES CANDY (USA)
AKCUPI Reg. No. 5SH00001
Breeder: GLORIA BLACKBURN
Owner: BERNIE REPALBOR
Address: 55 SCHOOL ST GRACE VILLAGE QUEZON CITY

SHIH TZU FEMALE GOLD & WHITE
Date Whelped: 17 May 1997
Foreign Reg. No.: AKC TN566383/01
Microchip No.:

Sire
AM CH MING DYNASTY'S SILK TEDDY
AKC TN036360/07
GOLD & WHITE

AM CH MING DYNASTY'S SILK TRADER
AKC TC751500
LIVER & WHITE

SHANEL KARYON CHATTY COWGIRL
AKC TM459656/01
GOLD & WHITE

AM CH GUNNING'S ON THE MAKE O' LOWREN
AKC TC452416 GOLD & WHITE

AM CH MING DYNASTY'S CHINESE SILK
AKC TC149592 GOLD & WHITE

AM CH KARYON SHANEL WESTERN WONDER
AKC TC777962 GOLD & WHITE

SHANEL'S CHATTY CATHY TU-CHU
AKC TC948710 GOLD & WHITE

AM CH LOUWAN'S REBEL ROUSER
AKC TB754162 GOLD & WHITE
AM CH GUNNING'S THE EIGHTH WONDER
AKC TB998791
AM CH LAINEE SIGMUND FLOYD
AKC TB439595 GOLD & WHITE OFA80
AM CH GUNNING'S TYPOGRAFICAL ERRER
AKC TB792955
AM CH GUNNING'S IT'S A WONDER
AKC TC586298 GOLD & WHITE
WINGATE'S KARYON POLLYANNA
AKC TC580000
AM CH REGAL'S DR DOLITTLE
AKC TC090212 GOLD & WHITE
AM CH TU CHU'S REACHED THE LIMIT
AKC TC489165 GOLD & WHITE

Dam
AM CH MISHSAR MING DYNASTY IMPULSE
AKC TM978122/02
GOLD & WHITE

AM/CAN CH TU CHU'S SKY'S THE LIMIT JE
AKC TC446058
GOLD & WHITE CKC 1026552

MING DYNASTY MISHSAR'S RUFFLE
AKC TM759919/01
GOLD & WHITE

AM CH TU CHU'S YOU ONLY LIVE TWICE
AKC TC198627 GOLD & WHITE

AM CH TU CHU'S MESMERIZED
AKC TC166194 GOLD & WHITE

AM CH CHAR-NO'S STARLORD AT DAWN
AKC TD262957 GOLD & WHITE

AM CH MING DYNASTY'S SILK RUFFLES
AKC TD100343 GOLD & WHITE

AM CH TU CHU GOLDEN HAPPINES MARJA
AKC TB922874
AM CH TU CHU'S FOR YOUR EYES ONLY
AKC TC021158
AM CH REGAL'S JACK N' THE BOX
AKC TB627309
GUNNING'S KIKI DEE
AKC TB803881
AM CH PE-KAE'S SAM-SUN
AKC TC519970
CHAR-NO'S CHRISMA
AKC TC860845

The Asian Kennel Club Union of the Philippines, Inc. certifies that this pedigree was compiled from official Stud Book records on 19 May 2008 Authorized Signature

CERTIFIED PEDIGREE & REGISTRATION CERTIFICATE

Decoding Your Dog's Certificate

Do you know what a "red mark," "green mark," HOF, etc. even mean? Do you actually know how to read your dog's papers? We help you decipher your dog's certificate and understand what it actually tells you about your dog.

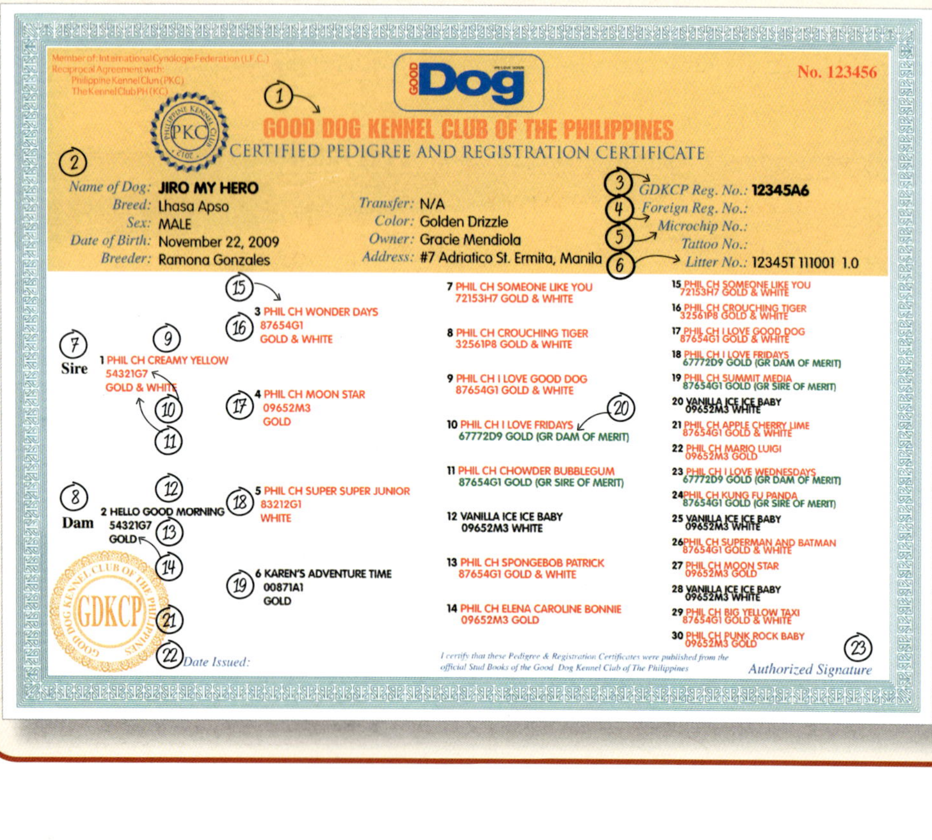

Member of: International Cynologie Federation (I.F.C.)
Reciprocal Agreement with:
Philippine Kennel Clun (PKC)
The Kennel Club PH (KC)

GOOD Dog

No. 123456

(1) GOOD DOG KENNEL CLUB OF THE PHILIPPINES
CERTIFIED PEDIGREE AND REGISTRATION CERTIFICATE

(2)
Name of Dog: **JIRO MY HERO**
Breed: Lhasa Apso
Sex: MALE
Date of Birth: November 22, 2009
Breeder: Ramona Gonzales

Transfer: N/A
Color: Golden Drizzle
Owner: Gracie Mendiola
Address: #7 Adriatico St. Ermita, Manila

(3) *GDKCP Reg. No.:* **12345A6**
(4) *Foreign Reg. No.:*
(5) *Microchip No.:*
Tattoo No.:
(6) *Litter No.:* 12345T 111001 1.0

(7) Sire (9)
1 PHIL CH CREAMY YELLOW
54321G7 (10)
GOLD & WHITE (11)

(8) Dam (12)
2 HELLO GOOD MORNING
54321G7 (13)
GOLD (14)

(15)
(16) 3 PHIL CH WONDER DAYS
87654G1
GOLD & WHITE

(17) 4 PHIL CH MOON STAR
09652M3
GOLD

(18) 5 PHIL CH SUPER SUPER JUNIOR
83212G1
WHITE

(19) 6 KAREN'S ADVENTURE TIME
00871A1
GOLD

7 PHIL CH SOMEONE LIKE YOU
72153H7 GOLD & WHITE

8 PHIL CH CROUCHING TIGER
32561P8 GOLD & WHITE

9 PHIL CH I LOVE GOOD DOG
87654G1 GOLD & WHITE

10 PHIL CH I LOVE FRIDAYS (20)
67772D9 GOLD (GR DAM OF MERIT)

11 PHIL CH CHOWDER BUBBLEGUM
87654G1 GOLD (GR SIRE OF MERIT)

12 VANILLA ICE ICE BABY
09652M3 WHITE

13 PHIL CH SPONGEBOB PATRICK
87654G1 GOLD & WHITE

14 PHIL CH ELENA CAROLINE BONNIE
09652M3 GOLD

15 PHIL CH SOMEONE LIKE YOU
72153H7 GOLD & WHITE

16 PHIL CH CROUCHING TIGER
32561P8 GOLD & WHITE

17 PHIL CH I LOVE GOOD DOG
87654G1 GOLD & WHITE

18 PHIL CH I LOVE FRIDAYS
67772D9 GOLD (GR DAM OF MERIT)

19 PHIL CH SUMMIT MEDIA
87654G1 GOLD (GR SIRE OF MERIT)

20 VANILLA ICE ICE BABY
09652M3 WHITE

21 PHIL CH APPLE CHERRY LIME
87654G1 GOLD & WHITE

22 PHIL CH MARIO LUIGI
09652M3 GOLD

23 PHIL CH I LOVE WEDNESDAYS
67772D9 GOLD (GR DAM OF MERIT)

24 PHIL CH KUNG FU PANDA
87654G1 GOLD (GR SIRE OF MERIT)

25 VANILLA ICE ICE BABY
09652M3 WHITE

26 PHIL CH SUPERMAN AND BATMAN
87654G1 GOLD & WHITE

27 PHIL CH MOON STAR
09652M3 GOLD

28 VANILLA ICE ICE BABY
09652M3 WHITE

29 PHIL CH BIG YELLOW TAXI
87654G1 GOLD & WHITE

30 PHIL CH PUNK ROCK BABY
09652M3 GOLD

GOOD DOG KENNEL CLUB OF THE PHILIPPINES GDKCP (21)

(22) *Date Issued:*

I certify that these Pedigree & Registration Certificates were published from the official Stud Books of the Good Dog Kennel Club of The Philippines

(23) Authorized Signature

1 The name of the kennel club

2 Basic information about the dog: his name, breed, color, date of birth (or date whelped), owner's name and address, breeder's name
Note that the breeder and the owner aren't always the same.

3 The dog's registration number with the kennel club

4 If he also belongs to a foreign kennel club, he will have a Foreign Registration Number.

5 If he has been microchipped, he will have a Microchip Number.

6 This refers to the Litter Number, or how many litters the dam and kennel has had, how many pups were born, and how many survived in that specific litter.

7 The father is called the sire.

8 The mother is called the dam.

9 This is the name of your dog's father.

10 This is your dog's father's registration number.
If the dog is registered to a foreign kennel club, he will use that club's registration number.

11 This is the color of your dog's father.

12 This is the name of your dog's mother.

13 This is your dog's mother's registration number.

14 This is the color of your dog's mother.
The color is noted for each of your dog's ancestors so you will have an idea what the dominant color of your dog's offsprings might be.

15 If the dog is a champion, his name and details will be printed in red (this is what they refer to when they use the term "red mark") and there will be a mention of it before his name.
Ex. PHIL CH – Philippine Champion, AM CH – American Champion, PHIL / CAN CH – the dog is both a Philippine and Canadian Champion
For a more comprehensive list, refer to the next page.

16 This is your dog's paternal grandfather.

17 This is your dog's paternal grandmother.

18 This is your dog's maternal grandfather.

19 This is your dog's maternal grandmother.
Every time you move one column to the right, you are tracing your dog's ancestry back one generation. Note that the sire or father will always have his name on top and the dam or mother will always have her name at the bottom.

20 GR DAM OF MERIT or GR SIRE OF MERIT
For a dog to be a sire of merit, he should have produced eight champion pups. He does not need to be a champion himself. For a dog to be a dam of merit, she should have produced five champion pups.
If the name on the list is printed in two colors (red and green), it means that the dog is both a champion and a dam or sire of merit. If the name is printed in all red, she or he is a champion but not a dam or sire of merit. If the name on the certificate is all green, she or he is a dam or sire of merit, but not a champion.

21 The official seal of the kennel or club

22 The date the certificate was issued

23 Authorized Signature
Signed by the corporate secretary or, in the absence of the secretary, the general manager or any board member

PCCI Point System

Philippine Champion (PHIL CH)

A dog needs to accumulate 15 points won under at least three different judges. Among these 15 points must be two majors (a win of three or more points) each taken under a different judge.

Philippine Grand Champion (PHIL GR CH)

A dog needs 25 points after its championship, won under at least five different judges. Among these 25 points must be at least three majors (a win of three or more points) each taken under a different judge.

Philippine Hall Of Famer (PHIL HOF)

A dog needs 100 points after its championship and must have won at least five group placements.

A dog starts winning championship points when it is adjudged Winners Dog or Winners Bitch. The maximum and minimum number of points that a dog can win in a breed competition is five points and one point, respectively, and points are awarded on the basis of a scale depending on the number of dogs in competition (see Tables 1 and 2). Thus, if the number of entries in a breed competition ranges from two to six, it falls in Category F and the championship points which can be awarded is indicated in the leftmost column. Table 2 indicates which breeds fall within the categories. These tables are periodically reviewed and modified as necessary.

International Champion

A dog needs four CACIB (no matter the number of dogs competing) taken from four different judges from three different countries. A dog should be at least 15 months old.

CACIB stands for Certificats d'Aptitude au Championnat International de Beauté or International Beauty Champion. CACIB certificate will only be available or awarded during FCI dog shows.

Dam Of Merit

A female dog should have produced five champions. (She doesn't necessarily need to be a champion herself.)

Grand Dam Of Merit (GR DAM OF MERIT)

A female dog should have produced eight champions. (She doesn't necessarily need to be a champion herself.)

Sire Of Merit

A male dog should have produced eight champions. (He doesn't necessarily need to be a champion himself.)

Grand Sire Of Merit (GR SIRE OF MERIT)

A male dog should have produced 16 champions. (He doesn't necessarily need to be a champion himself.)

Table 1. Scale of Points Per Entry Category

Points	Category A	Category B	Category C	Category D	Category E	Category F
5	17-up	14-up	12-up	9-up	7	6
4	14-16	11-13	9-11	7-8	6	5
3	11-13	9-10	7-8	6	5	4
2	7-10	5-8	5-6	4-5	3-4	3
1	4-6	3-4	3-4	2-3	2	2

Table 2. Breeds in Entry Category

Category A	Category B	Category C	Category D	Category E	Category F
			Beagle Chihuahua (SC)	Shih Tzu Labrador Ret. French Bulldog	All other breeds recognized by PCCI

Natural Balance

CHAPTER 3

Nutrition

Dogs are notorious for being enthusiastic eating machines—put any type of food in front of them or within their vicinity and you can almost be sure that it will get eaten, whatever it is. They'll beg for a taste of whatever you're snacking on or chew on an inedible object they found lying on the floor, prompting dog owners across the ages to yell, "What's that in your mouth? NO! Don't eat that!"

Since dogs will happily eat anything they can sink their teeth into, some people hardly think twice about the kind of food they feed their dog, but as a responsible dog owner, you need to make an informed decision about the kind of food you give him. You should make sure that it's something that will contribute to your dog's overall health.

Nutrition for Puppies

Introduce solid food once your puppy has been weaned from his mother's milk, which is usually done between four to six weeks of age. Ideally, by the time he is six to eight weeks old, he should be eating solid food. Giving your dog milk or a milk supplement is optional, unless the breeder tells you to do so because the puppy still takes milk; in which case, you can stop once your puppy reaches three months of age. Make sure you get a complete high-quality and all-natural dog food for a puppy two months and older; the dog food label should indicate that the food is complete and balanced, as opposed to some canned brands that are merely supplemental. Moisten his dog food with water to make it easier for your newly weaned puppy to chew.

You can get your puppy started on good eating habits by scheduling the feedings, paying careful attention to the time when you feed him and sticking to that schedule every day, as opposed to feeding him at random hours throughout the day. This is a good way to train your dog when to expect his meals and get into a normal routine. Your puppy should initially be fed up to four times a day. After he hits eight weeks of age, you can begin feeding him twice a day. When your puppy starts teething, expect him to be less enthusiastic about eating; you may need to moisten his food with water. You can also soak his food in some lactose-free milk or dog milk substitute; never use regular milk, since most dogs are lactose-intolerant.

Your little puppy will greatly benefit from a diet rich in protein, which is a vital key to his growth and development, along with nutrients like calcium and iron. Puppy food is usually packed with all these nutrients, so you wouldn't have to give your puppy any supplements unless he has special needs or it is otherwise recommended by your vet. Make sure to ask your vet during the first checkup; any supplements will depend on your puppy's needs or the brand of dog food he is on.

The label on your puppy's food will usually indicate the recommended serving size based on volume (cu) or weight (grams), so check which one is appropriate for your puppy and stick to it unless your vet recommends otherwise.

As your puppy grows older, ask your vet when you can switch to feeding him food that is suited to adult dogs. You can make the transition by checking the recommendations of the dog food manufacturer. It also depends on the age and breed size of your dog. The general rule is to switch at around 10 months to one year old, but special considerations are given to teacup and giant breeds. Be sure to check with your vet before making any changes to your puppy's food or his eating schedule.

You should never overfeed your puppy

in an effort to boost his growth rate. You want him to grow at the proper rate, for starters. Furthermore, his food intake doesn't determine how big he could grow anyway. Overfeeding could also affect his digestion, lead to unwanted weight gain, or a metabolic disease called panosteitis or growing pains in large-breed dogs.

Nutrition for Adult Dogs

At this age, you should have already found the right food for your dog and he should be on a well-balanced diet. You'll know he's eating the right food when he's healthy, has a good and thick coat, ample energy levels, and has no adverse reactions to anything you're feeding him.

You can choose the right food—preferably one that's suitable for all life stages or for adult maintenance—and the ideal feeding schedule for your adult dog by paying attention to his lifestyle. Is your dog active, the kind who already wants to go for a walk even if he just went for one? Or is he perfectly happy lounging around on the floor or any available lap in the vicinity? A lapdog won't need the same amount of food as a dog who gets regular exercise, and should eat about 10 percent less than the recommended serving.

Your adult dog should be fed twice a day, although there are dogs who can get by with only one meal a day. Make sure that there's a right balance of protein, carbohydrates, fiber, and fat in his meal. Studying the labels on the dog food packaging will give you an idea whether or not your dog is getting a well-balanced meal. You should look at the ingredients and sources of the nutrients. If you're feeding your dog home-cooked food, your vet can provide you with guidelines on food combinations that will achieve the optimum nutrient levels for your pooch.

Measuring how much food to give your dog, as well as considering the amount of protein and calories that are in it, helps in keeping your dog at his optimum weight. If your dog is overweight, switch to feeding him low-calorie dog food and ask your vet to come up with a weight-loss plan. An overweight dog can lose extra pounds with a combination of regular exercise and reduced food intake. For severely overweight dogs, you might want to cut out treats altogether. Sometimes, though, a dog's weight issue may be due to a hormonal problem and will require treatment by a veterinarian.

Nutrition for a Pregnant Dog

Having puppies can be tough on your dog, so you have to make sure that she is well-fed and healthy. A dog's gestation period typically lasts up to 65 days, so your dog's meals should be suited to her needs throughout her pregnancy. You have to make sure she eats a high-quality dog food complete with all the necessary nutrients. During the early weeks of her pregnancy, you don't have to give her extra food. Pregnancy is diagnosed by ultrasound at around 30 days at the earliest, and supplements and dietary changes are introduced by the fourth week or a little later, as your dog's weight increases by 25 to 30 percent.

When your dog is pregnant, you should add one more serving to her food and make sure it has a higher protein content. Check dog food labels as well to learn the recommended amount for pregnant dogs. You can also add one extra feeding per day, with about a 25 percent increase if your dog is pregnant or lactating. As soon as she is diagnosed pregnant, you will need to start feeding puppy food to your pregnant dog or food with more protein and fat until the puppies are weaned, since this will help in nourishing her litter. Active-lifestyle dog food is also recommended.You can switch back to her regular food serving after the puppies are weaned and are no longer suckling.

A pregnant dog must also get multivitamins and supplements with folic acid and calcium

VET'S TIP

"I recommend that a pregnant dog be on food with higher protein and fat during her pregnancy and while she's nursing. Switch from regular adult maintenance dog food to either the puppy or active-lifestyle variant of your dog food. Also remember to give her pre- and post-natal supplements."

Margarita Carpio, D.V.M.

for the duration of her pregnancy and until her puppies are weaned, but remember that any supplements your dog might need should be recommended by your vet.

Nutrition for Senior Dogs

As your dog grows older, you're going to see less and less of the energetic dog who would run around and wag his tail at the mere mention of taking a walk. Your senior dog will prefer shorter walks, longer naps, and to hang around the house watching the day go by. His metabolism slows down considerably as well. You might also notice that he doesn't have as much of an appetite as he used to.

Because your senior dog is less active, there are some adjustments that you should makes with his food, starting with reducing the amount of fat and protein. Find a dog food made specifically for senior or less-active dogs. Less protein means less work for his organs. Aside from the amount of protein, you also have to consider the quality of the protein in his dog food or that you are integrating into his meals. Food containing excessive or poor-quality protein will lead to more waste products which can damage or overwork his kidneys. Keep in mind that the kidneys and the heart are the most common vital organs affected by age. The wear and tear of these organs take place much more quickly, so you really have to choose your senior dog's food wisely.

The metabolism of older dogs also tends to slow down as they age, making them prone to obesity. Reducing your dog's calorie intake can help keep weight gain at bay. Weight control is especially important for dogs who are suffering from joint problems and heart disease.

You can also opt to feed him specialty diets which are designed to decrease the workload of specific vital organs. Such diets work by supporting the functions of each organ and supplementing them with specific nutrients to enhance their function and replace any deficits. You'll need veterinary prescriptions for these diets, however, so be sure to ask your vet. For the most part, you should follow the guidelines written on the manufacturer's label regarding the right amount of food to feed your senior dog. Any modifications should be prescribed by your vet.

There are diets for each life stage, so make sure you read the labels of the food you're getting for your dog. Alternatively, you can prepare home-cooked meals for your senior dog; have your vet assist you in coming up with well-balanced meals. Be careful when tweaking the meals and making substitutions, since any changes could lead to nutritional deficiencies; ask your vet for help if changes have to be made and if he or she can recommend ingredients which have a similar nutritional content that can be used as substitutes.

You may also want to hold back on the treats. Occasional treats are okay, but remember that they mostly contain fat, sugar, and empty calories. Your senior dog will need something more beneficial, like supplements that boost the function of his heart and kidneys, detoxify his liver, improve blood circulation, or protect and lubricate his joints. Natural and pharmacological preparations are widely available, but consult your vet before giving any to your dog.

If your dog has any health problems, such as diabetes or liver disease, you should ask your vet to suggest a diet that will meet your dog's needs without having a negative effect on his health. You want to make sure you're giving him food that will either help treat his condition or keep it from worsening.

If you notice any unusual changes, talk to your vet to determine whether these changes are naturally occurring due to age or are symptoms of a disease. You will most likely notice that your senior dog's appetite is no longer what it used to be and that he will start to seem disinterested in food. Ask your vet for dietary changes you should make for your dog so you can get him to eat, and have him checked as well to learn if his lack of appetite or any other changes are not due to some underlying condition.

Dealing with Food Allergies and Intolerance

You might think that all dog food is created equal and that they're perfectly suited to every dog. Ideally, that should be the case, but there are instances when your dog is allergic to the ingredients in the food or is suffering from food intolerance. Your dog isn't being a finicky eater—he's really reacting to something in the food you're giving him, and making changes can help him enjoy his meals and provide him with the right nutrients.

When humans are allergic to food, we exhibit a variety of symptoms, from swelling to breaking out in hives to having difficulty breathing, among others. Dogs with food allergies, however, won't be sneezing and wheezing—their allergies manifest on their skin. Your dog may break out in hives, have skin rashes, and be scratching incessantly; he may also exhibit chronic ear inflammation. Of course, these symptoms can also indicate other illnesses, such as an allergy to flea bites, so make sure that all other conditions are ruled out before concluding that your dog has a food allergy.

If his food is the cause of his allergy, your vet will put him on an elimination diet, which involves removing certain food items from your dog's diet and then gradually reintroducing them to his meals until the cause of his food allergy is determined. Your dog will then be put on a special diet for a certain period of time, which will include ingredients that weren't present in the meal he used to eat. Such diets could use either commercial food or homemade food. Whichever one your vet recommends, you should to keep other kinds of food and treats away from your dog until the cause of the allergy has been identified. Remember that food allergies can develop over time, and that your dog might even become allergic to something that he's been eating regularly.

If your dog is experiencing food

intolerance, however, his reactions will be somewhat different. Your dog may have loose stools or he may become flatulent, among other gastrointestinal symptoms. In extreme cases, your dog might even start vomiting. In the case of food intolerance, your dog really cannot digest what you're feeding him. Your vet can also put him on an elimination diet. Once the offending ingredient has been identified, he or she can recommend alternative diets.

You can't prevent food allergies and intolerance, since these are things your dog is already predisposed to. The best you can do is to be aware when your dog is having a different reaction to his food and to refrain from feeding him foods that his body doesn't agree with.

Choosing the Right Dog Food

Feeding your dog doesn't take a lot of effort. All you really need to do is grab a can of dog food and pop the tin open, or scoop up the right amount of dry dog food and pour it into your dog's food bowl. You just have to remember to feed him at specific times of the day, check if your dog is eating, and put the food away once he's had enough or isn't showing interest in it anymore. But you have to make sure to get the right dog food. Do your homework: research, ask around, read the label, and consult with your vet before you zero in on one specific brand. There are a lot of differences in the content although they may look the same. Your vet can help narrow your choice down to some brands. Mostly it will depend on your budget and your dog's specific needs.

Preparing Home-cooked Meals for Your Dog

Feeding your dog home-cooked meals definitely has its advantages. First of all, since you're the one preparing it, you know exactly what goes into the food. Plus, home-cooked meals are more natural and have no preservatives, unless you use ingredients containing preservatives. If your dog suffers from allergies or issues with his digestive system, home-cooked meals may be a better choice, since they can be tailored to meet your dog's health requirements. Some dogs don't respond well to commercially available or processed dog food, and food cooked specifically to meet their needs may be much better for them.

This puts a lot of responsibility on your shoulders, however, since your dog's health and nutrition are completely in your hands and you have to be sure that what you are feeding him really is good for him. That is why you have to ask your vet for information on what food items you can cook for your dog as well as seek advice on how to prepare well-balanced meals for him. Your vet will be able to help you determine how to achieve the perfect combination of fat, protein, calcium, and all the other nutrients you will need to incorporate into his meals.

You need to remember that a home-cooked meal is not the same as leftovers, *adobo, sinigang,* or hotdog. The meals have to consist of human-grade ingredients, minus the spices and seasonings.

Additionally, you have to keep in mind that cooking for your dog requires a lot of time and effort on your part. You want to make sure that he gets his meals on time, so you must prepare and cook his food ahead of his feeding schedule. Making home-cooked meals for your dog certainly takes more work, so you also have to consider whether it's an option you're willing and able to take.

Feeding Don'ts

Some dog owners say that their dog is a picky eater. In most cases, this has nothing to do with the food you're serving, but with the feeding rituals you have established. For example, your dog becomes a picky eater if you expose him to a wide array of food, including human food. You might be thinking that you're teaching your dog to become a more sophisticated eater by going beyond dog food, but what's actually happening is that you're making his palate and tastes more complicated, which causes him to develop a sweet tooth or a preference for treats.

Some dogs also tend to dawdle during mealtimes, eating only a little at a time instead of finishing their food during their set mealtimes. You can work on this behavior by making sure you only leave food out for your dog for 15 to 20 minutes, then taking it away whether or not he's done eating—just make sure you don't take it away while your dog is still eating. Leaving his food out for an indeterminate amount of time, or "free feeding," is a bad idea because the dog will assume that food is always readily available.

There are also dogs who eat only when they're fed a certain way—you might know a few dog owners who have dogs who won't eat unless they're hand-fed. Some people say that hand-feeding a dog helps you bond with your pet, but when you find yourself hand-feeding your dog every mealtime and feeling frustrated because he won't eat without you by his side, you will realize that you haven't trained him to become more fond of you—your dog has only become incapable of eating on his own and has trained *you* to serve him. You want him to be able to eat even when you're not there to feed him yourself or to supervise him—you don't want him to go hungry when you're at work, off on vacation, or when you're coming home late from the office. A qualified dog trainer will be able to help in correcting this particular behavior as well as teach you how to instill proper eating habits in your dog.

What Not to Feed Your Dog

Ever think your dog might be getting tired of eating the same food and treats day in and day out, so you begin feeding him food from your plate and passing him different treats every now and then? Stop right there. While there is such a thing as food fatigue in dogs, which causes a loss of appetite, that is not the solution. Maybe all you need to do is heat a tablespoon of canned dog food and add it as a topping to his kibble. Consult with your vet and ask for advice on what you can do if your dog is suffering from food fatigue. Do not give him human food that you are not 100 percent sure is safe for him. Do not assume that what's good for you must be good for him, too. There are certain foods that could lead to illness and even death when ingested by dogs. Even onions, which we eat regularly, are harmful to dogs.

Here's a short list of some of the foods that can be harmful or even toxic to dogs.

1 **Chocolate.** It can stimulate your dog's cardiac and nervous system, as well as cause him to vomit and have seizures.

2 **Grapes and raisins.** While they're great sources of antioxidants for humans, they can cause kidney failure in dogs.

3 **Onion.** This can damage your dog's red blood cells and result in anemia.

4 **Caffeine.** It causes hypertension, an elevated heart rate, tremors, seizures, and collapse.

5 **Table scraps.** 99 percent of Filipino pet owners still feed their pets table scraps even though leftovers clearly have no place in their diet.

6 **Fatty foods.** These are attractive and dangerous for both humans and dogs. Fatty foods can also cause pancreatitis in dogs.

7 **Sodium.** It's a good idea to keep chips away from your dog. Too much salt can cause sodium ion poisoning as well as vomiting and diarrhea.

8 **Alcohol.** Dogs are more sensitive to ethanol than humans. Alcohol intoxication causes vomiting and disorientation, and in extreme cases, coma, seizures, and death.

9 **Macadamia nuts.** These cause muscle tremors, an inability to stand, depression, and vomiting, symptoms which appear 12 hours after your dog has eaten macadamia nuts. It is still unknown what component in macadamia nuts makes them toxic to dogs.

Keep these out of your dog's reach and remind others about your dog's food restrictions.

Providing proper nourishment for your dog at every stage of his life is absolutely crucial to his development, which is why you have to learn what types of food your dog should eat and which ones you should keep away from him, and to understand how food affects his health.

Choose all-natural pet food
for a healthier and happier baby.

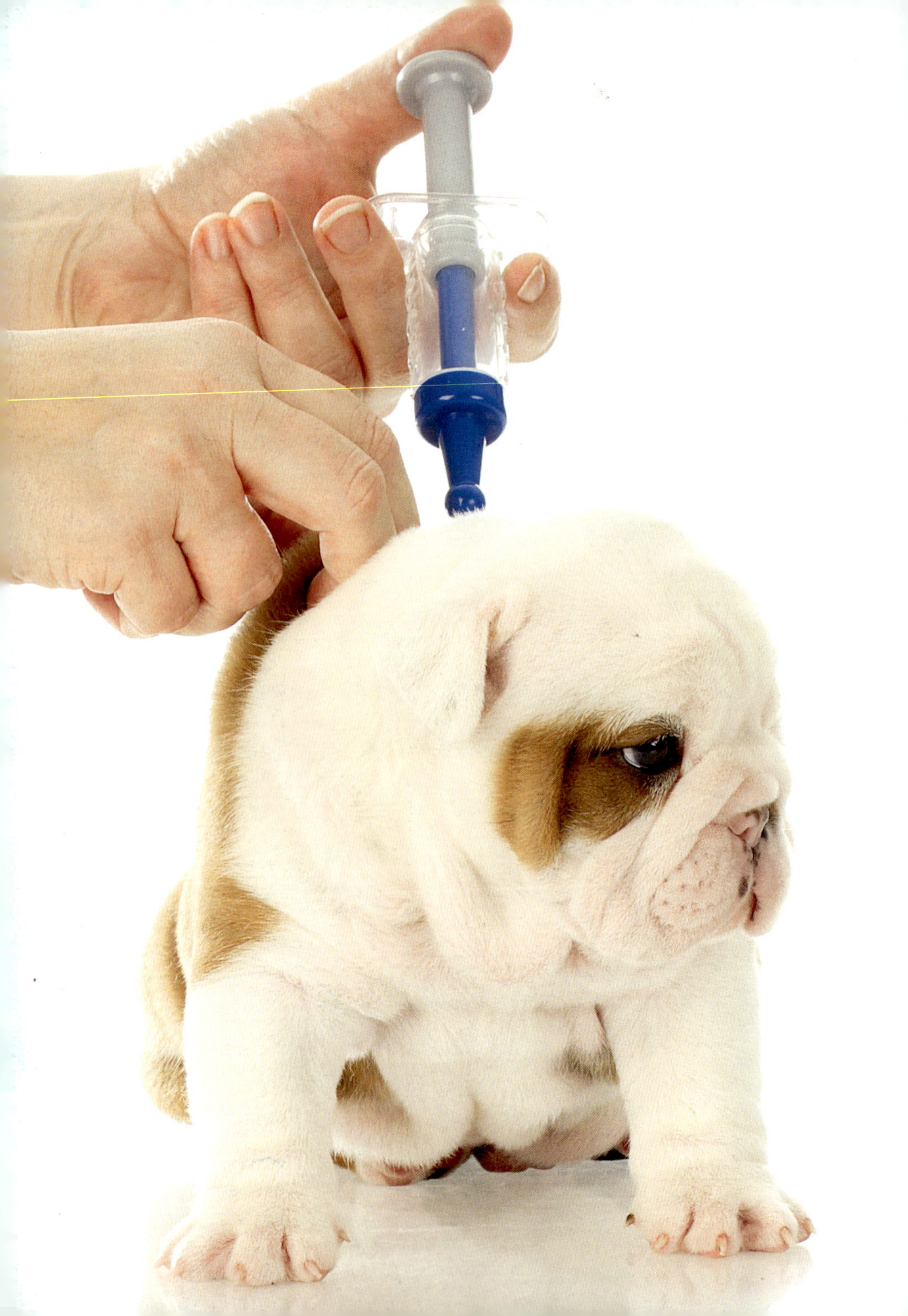

CHAPTER 4

Healthcare

Owning a dog doesn't just mean you finally have a cute, furry companion to keep you entertained and liven up your home. It basically means that you're now responsible for a living, breathing creature. So you need to ensure that he remains healthy under your care. You are responsible for keeping your dog in the best condition at every stage of his life.

Healthcare for Puppies

When you first get your puppy, you should take him to the vet right away. The sooner he receives a vet's attention, the easier it will be for your vet to address any health issue he may have and to complete a vaccination and deworming program. Do your research to find the right vet for you and your puppy. Remember, he or she will be your partner in raising your dog, so it's vital that you find one whom you can trust. During the first visit, the vet will check your puppy's weight, examine his arms and legs for proper conformation, and see if his coat is healthy. Your vet will run his or her hands throughout your dog's body feeling for any possible lumps, bumps, or external parasites. Your vet will also take a stool sample for a fecal examination to see if he has any worms, parasites, or bacteria. He or she will also check your puppy's ears for dirt as well as examine the color and the volume of earwax; excessive earwax is a sign of ear mites or a yeast infection.

The first visit is also the perfect time for you to ask for advice on what you should be feeding your puppy, as well as health issues you should expect. Any follow-up visits will involve monitoring, and you can then discuss your puppy's bowel movements as well as his eating habits. Usually, a puppy would have already adjusted to the food the breeder has been feeding him, but changes may be recommended, such as switching to premium-quality dog food and supplements.

You should take advantage of your puppy's visit by asking questions you might have about your puppy's health. Below are some frequently asked questions that you should ask your vet.

- Please provide suggestions for potty training and basic obedience.
- What should I feed my dog, how often, and how much food should I give him?
- What food should my dog never eat?
- What can I expect after a vaccine is given to my dog?
- What basic first-aid steps should I take for common health concerns?
- How often should a vet visit be scheduled?
- What supplements should my puppy take?
- What toys are safe for my puppy?

You should make a list of your dog's habits, diet, and behavior and show it to your vet. He or she will be able to help you if any changes have to be made.

Vaccinating Your Puppy

A complete and thorough vaccination and deworming program is imperative to your dog's health. Many canine viruses are fatal, and many of them are still highly prevalent in the country, compared to other countries where decades of vaccination have reduced the incidence of canine viral diseases. Here in the Philippines, these diseases remain in full force because pet owners have only recently become more informed about the proper vaccinations. The dense population here also makes infections more widespread.

When your puppy is vaccinated, he is exposed to the virus in the form of the vaccine, and his body will then produce antibodies that will protect him against that particular virus should he ever get infected with it. For puppies, a consecutive series of shots gradually builds protective immunity. Booster shots are given throughout the dog's life to make sure that he always has an adequate amount of antibodies in his immune system to fight off a viral infection.

Every veterinarian will have his or her own recommended vaccination plan or schedule based on the animal's age, breed, environment, and the owner's lifestyle. The following are the most common vaccines given during puppyhood (around two months to six months of age)

- DHLPPi or 5 in 1
- DHLPPi-C or 6 in 1
- DP- 2 in 1
- Bordetella vaccine
- Dermatophyte vaccine
- Rabies vaccine

A Brief Look at the Common Viruses Afflicting Dogs

Here are a few diseases that your dog needs to get vaccinated against.

DISTEMPER - an airborne viral disease of the lungs, intestines, and nerves that can infect puppies and dogs of all ages
SYMPTOMS: on-and-off fever, thick yellowish eye discharge, watery nasal discharge, diarrhea, paralysis and twitching, inappetence, "hard pad" or thickening of foot pads or nose

HEPATITIS - a viral disease of the liver that can also affect the kidneys and lungs
SYMPTOMS: fever, depression, eye discharge, abdominal pain and vomiting, edema of neck, head, or body

LEPTOSPIROSIS - a bacterial disease of the urinary tract that affects the kidney and liver; common source of infection is contaminated rat urine. Humans can also be affected by this bacteria.
SYMPTOMS: fever, depression, anorexia, eye and nasal discharge, jaundice or yellowing, acetone breath or mouth ulcers in cases of renal failure

PARAINFLUENZA - a virus that causes mild infection of the respiratory tract
SYMPTOMS: dry coughing, nasal discharge, retching that produces mucus

PARVOVIRUS - a viral disease of the intestines that affects the gut lining, which causes bloody diarrhea
SYMPTOMS: fever, anorexia, bloody stool, vomiting

RABIES - a viral disease affecting the brain and is fatal to humans and other warm-blooded animals
SYMPTOMS: excessive salivation, anorexia, change in behavior (aggression or reclusion, nervousness)

CORONAVIRUS - a viral disease of the intestines that causes diarrhea and predisposes the animal to other viral and bacterial pathogens
SYMPTOMS: diarrhea, vomiting, anorexia

BORDETELLA - a highly infectious bacterial infection of the upper respiratory system (kennel cough)
SYMPTOMS: dry, harsh cough accompanied by gagging

VACCINATION SCHEDULE Puppies (aged six weeks to one year)

- **Six – eight weeks:** First and second puppy shot (DHLPPi) + Corona
- **10 – 12 weeks:** Third and fourth puppy shot (DHLPPi) + Corona + Bordetella (twice)
- **16 - 24 weeks:** Third puppy shot (DHLPPi)
- **Over three months:** Rabies vaccine (repeat annually)
- **Six months:** First heartworm test and prevention

Protecting Your Puppy from Parasites

Antiparasitic medicines are frequently given to rid our dogs of parasites, many of which lurk visibly or invisibly on and inside the canine body. Oral dewormers are given early in life (three to six weeks) to kill any worms that may have been contracted from the mother's blood, milk, or the surroundings. Dewormers are administered two weeks after the first treatment to destroy eggs that have not been killed during the first treatment. Tablets and liquid suspensions are the most common form of these anti-nematocidal or anti-worm medicines. The most common anti-worm medications can kill roundworms, hookworms, tapeworm, and even immature heartworm. Oral, injectable, and spot-on preparations are available, so make sure to ask your vet to give you an appropriate recommendation.

DEWORMING SCHEDULE

- **four to six weeks:** first deworming
- **six to eight weeks:** second deworming

Taking Care of Your Puppy's Teeth

His teeth begin growing when he's between six and eight weeks old, and the entire set will be complete once he hits three to six months old. This set will then fall out one at a time, starting with the front teeth, followed by those at the sides, then the back, and finally the sharp canines. These will be replaced by permanent teeth when your dog is around eight to 10 months old. When your puppy begins teething, get him some good chew toys. Select chew toys that are appropriate for his size and age, and ones that won't break up into small pieces that he could swallow and which could cause intestinal blockage.

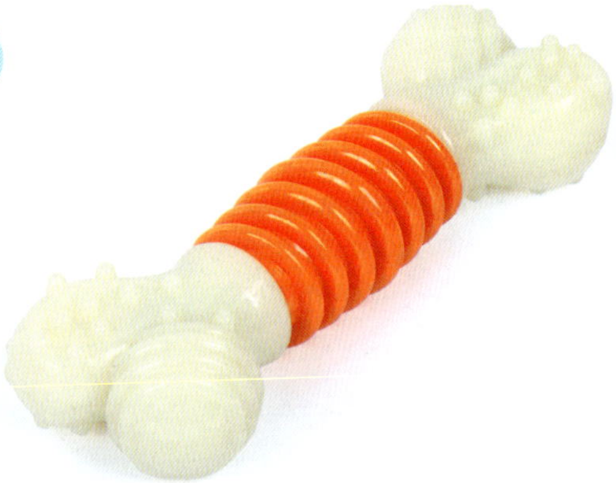

This is also the right time for your puppy to start getting used to having his mouth and teeth handled, and for you to start learning how to do this correctly, too. You simply have to tilt your puppy's head up carefully, lift the upper and lower lips, then gently touch the gums. This helps your puppy get accustomed to having his mouth handled, which is necessary for when you're going to brush his teeth or administer any medications in the future. Make sure to praise him a lot and pat him or give him a treat after he allows you to examine his mouth. Remember that your puppy should sit still all throughout, without nipping or chewing on your fingers.

Common Health Issues Affecting Puppies

The most common problems encountered in puppies are related to the integumentary (skin) and digestive systems because these systems aren't fully developed yet during the early stages of his life. During this time, he is still susceptible to skin infections and loose stools or indigestion. Fortunately, your vet can treat most of these easily. Your puppy can also outgrow these issues once his immune system is fully developed, but there is no guarantee. Sometimes there are issues, like certain allergies, that he may not outgrow and have to deal with for the rest of his life.

Keep in mind that this simply provides general information on possible health problems. Any diagnosis and treatment should be done by your vet.

Skin

PUPPY PYODERMA. Pus-filled, pimple-like bumps appear all over or on any part of your puppy's body, particularly on the belly, thighs, and the groin area.
CAUSE: Bacterial infection on your puppy's skin due to poor hygiene (beddings may always be soiled and not cleaned frequently) or the puppy's still-weak immune system.
TREATMENT: Scrub the affected area with an antibacterial soap or shampoo, and apply antimicrobial cream.

FUNGAL SKIN INFECTIONS. Puppies in particular are susceptible to ringworm, which is characterized by circular itchy lesions, white flakes on the surface of the skin, and hair loss on the affected area.
CAUSE: Dermatophytes like *Microsporum* and *Trichophyton*, fungi which live on dead skin tissues.
TREATMENT: Trim the fur around the affected area, give your puppy a bath with an antifungal shampoo, and apply an antifungal cream afterward. Keep the affected areas dry; aeration and exposure to the sun can help. You might also want to wash any towels, brushes, combs, and other grooming materials that have had contact with your puppy's skin to keep the infection from spreading.

URINE BURNS. These appear as red blisters near the vulva of female puppies or on the skin near the tip of the penis of male puppies, as well as on the belly.
CAUSE: These appear because your puppy can't groom himself well yet. Poor hygiene and wet and dirty beddings are also to blame.
TREATMENT: Wipe your dog's genital area clean and wash with water several times a day. Aerate his skin and protect it with extra virgin coconut oil or diaper rash cream. You can also give your puppy supplements like vitamins A, C, and E, which improve skin health and boost the immune system. Don't forget to change his beddings regularly.

Remember That, Like Babies, Puppies Need Lots of Sleep

Remind your children—and yourself—that your puppy is not a toy. A puppy who's running away from play and hiding in corners or under furniture may be getting stressed. From time to time, your puppy might fall asleep in your arm, and won't stir despite loud noises or probing. This certainly seems like a very cute image, but it actually means you have on your hands an overfatigued puppy with low sugar levels. So let your little puppy sleep and respect his need to sleep. Don't wake him just because you want to play with him.

Digestion

DIARRHEA Your puppy might have loose, watery, or pasty stool.

CAUSE: Sudden changes in food brands or too much treats can cause indigestion. Your puppy might have also eaten garbage or something inedible, or is suffering from an infection caused by a virus or bacteria.

TREATMENT: To prevent indigestion, new food should be introduced gradually. Mix one-quarter portion of the new food with three-quarter portion of old food on the first day. If stool is formed the next day, feed your dog equal portions of both food. In the next few days, add more and more of the new food. If your puppy produces soft, runny stool, give him food with the same portions as the day when his stool was formed. Increase the amount of the new food only when his stool is properly formed. Simple indigestion can also be treated with probiotics in the form of yogurt, lactose-free milk, paste, gels, tablets and capsules.

If your puppy's diarrhea goes on for too long (more than 48 hours) or if it spontaneously resolves without treatment but recurs after a day or two, and if your puppy shows other symptoms like fever, lethargy, and lack of appetite, take your puppy to the vet to rule out any other infectious causes.

HYPOGLYCEMIA This occurs commonly in teacup and toy breeds, and very young puppies, and is characterized by episodes of weakness and sleepiness, trembling or shaking after play or exercise. In severe cases, the dog may also have seizures and convulsions.

CAUSE: A puppy's undeveloped liver is unable to store glycogen, which leads to his body's energy stores being easily depleted.

PREVENTION AND TREATMENT: A puppy with a mild case of hypoglycemia can be given sugar water, corn syrup, or honey. Other options are dextrose powder preparations mixed with water and pasty commercial prepartions with molasses and vitamins, which can be given every few hours. Puppies with severe cases of hypoglycemia need immediate veterinary attention and intravenous dextrose.

Preparing Your Puppy for a Vet Exam

Going through a vet exam is something new for your puppy, and you want to make sure that the experience will be easy for him, for you, and for your vet. It always helps if your puppy is on his best behavior, as this is something he'll carry up to adulthood. You don't necessarily want him to learn how to stand still for a vet exam, but he should at least learn to become more patient and tolerant. Here are some ways for you to achieve this.

1. Place your puppy on a table in a standing position. Hold your puppy's collar at the nape of his neck with your right hand.

2. Initially, your puppy will stand in place for a while, but he may soon try to walk around or even jump off the table. Don't fuss over him if he does and be firm about keeping him still on the table. Don't let go if he starts struggling; otherwise, he will learn that struggling makes you let go. Hold him until he relaxes. Praise and pet him when he does. You can also give him a treat so he associates standing on the table with something good.

3. As he becomes more relaxed about being on the table, you can have other people come to touch him, run their hands all over him, and give him a treat afterward. Get him used to his paws being touched and examined. Open his mouth and look at his teeth. Look inside his ears. Stroke his tail. The initial contact should be brief. You should increase the duration and pressure gradually so your puppy gets used to it. Keep the interaction calm, relaxed, and enjoyable for him. One of the best times to do this is when he is tired and relaxed after a play session so he is less likely to struggle. Do this a few times every week and not just on the day of or before his visit to the vet.

At this age, you not only need to nurture your puppy physically, but also make sure he develops mentally and socially. He will need good food, proper veterinary attention, intellectual stimulation, and socialization with other dogs in order to grow into a healthy, happy, and balanced dog.

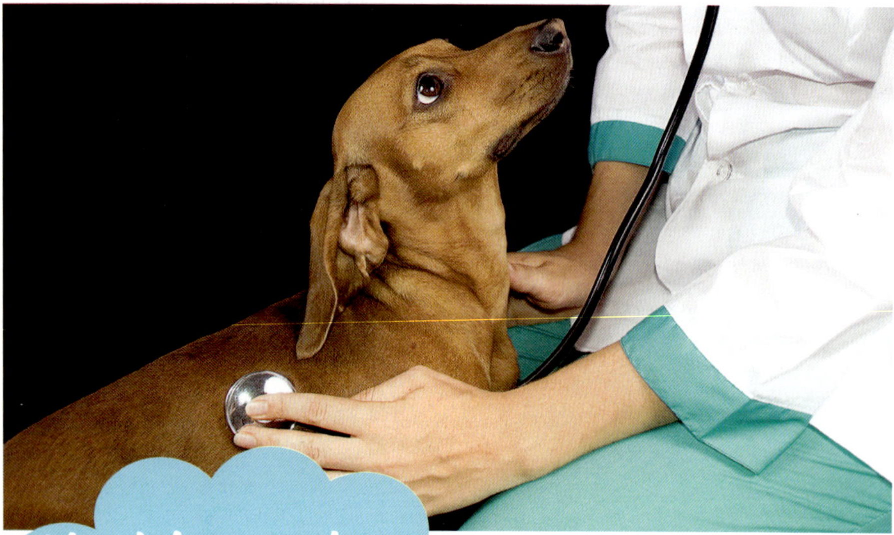

Healthcare for Adult Dogs

If you raised your puppy right, attending to his health requirements and giving him the right food and any necessary medical treatment, and your dog was blessed with good genes, you should have a healthy companion now. Dog owners find that adulthood is the easiest and most enjoyable stage in taking care of a dog. Your healthy, well-mannered dog is a joy to have around—and everyone feels the same way, too.

The initial series of shots given to your dog as a puppy will now be replaced by yearly shots and bi-annual visits to your veterinarian. By now, veterinary checkups are quick and thorough. If you were able to prepare your pooch to be handled by different people as a puppy, then going to the vet should now be a pleasant experience. If not, it's never too late to try to condition him; all it takes is some patience and consistent correction.

It's generally advisable to take your dog to the vet twice a year, even if your pooch appears to be healthy—you want your vet to confirm your observations or to check for any possible health problems. Depending on your lifestyle or your dog's overall health condition, your vet might ask you to come in for a checkup more frequently. A dog owner who goes to the beach or farm weekly will find that his or her dog has different health issues compared with a condo-dwelling dog who walks 15 minutes twice a day and stays indoors most of the time.

During adulthood, it is important that your dog gets sufficient exercise. Having a lean and well-muscled body will prevent or delay osteoarthritis or diabetes later on in his life. Exercise is also important for his mental well-being. Lack of exercise can manifest as hyperactivity, destructive behavior, excessive barking, and even aggression.

By now, your adult dog would have already outgrown his skin and tummy problems, unless he's been diagnosed with health issues such as allergies or atopic dermatitis. Such conditions cannot be cured, only managed. He should also be consuming a balanced diet which suits his digestive system and keeps him nourished.

You should also expect the following vaccines to be administered to your adult dog (one year and up) at this stage:

- Annual DHLPPi or 5-in-1 shots
- Quarterly deworming
- Annual heartworm prevention in the form of either monthly tablets, shots or spot-ons, or annual shots
- Annual Bordetella vaccine shots for kennel cough
- Annual rabies vaccine shots

Other optional vaccines:

- Bi-annual Leptospirosis vaccine
- Dermatophyte (fungal) vaccination
- Quarterly or Bi-annual deworming

Note:

Every practitioner may have his or her own recommendations regarding the vaccination schedule.

Inspecting Your Dog

Grooming is essential in keeping your dog healthy, because daily brushing can minimize shedding and stimulate the production of natural oils needed to keep the coat smooth, soft, and shiny. This also gives you a chance to check him for ticks, fleas, scabs, lumps, or bumps. When watching your dog playing or simply relaxing, be on the lookout as well for any odd behaviors that suggest discomfort or any unusual changes in his appearance. For example, while scratching is part of everyday dog behavior, enthusiastic scratching complete with vocalization or foot thumping could be a sign of either a pest attack or an allergy.

You need to do more than observe your dog for unusual symptoms—you have to get hands-on. Check him carefully once a week or while you're grooming him. Use the details below as guidelines when you're giving your dog a thorough inspection.

- EYES. They should be clear and bright, with no excessive discharge. The center of the eye should be black to dark brown. The dog shouldn't be blinking excessively.

- EARS. The underside of the ear flap should be light pink, not red and hot to the touch. The flap should be flat; any large bump between the skin of the ear flap is abnormal. The ears should not be foul-smelling, and your dog shouldn't be twitching his ears and scratching them constantly or tilting his head to one side. The natural color of earwax is light brown to yellow. Dark brown to yellow wax oozing from the ear, accompanied by head-shaking, may signal of an infection.

- **MOUTH.** He should have a complete set of teeth and show no signs of gum disease. His gums should be light pink; if the gum line (the area directly above or below a tooth) is red or bleeds easily during handling, he could have gingivitis or periodontal gum disease. The surface of each tooth should have no or minimal brown staining or tartar formation, and his teeth should be white, even-colored, and none of them loose or moving. His breath shouldn't be foul and offensive.

- **NECK.** It should be smooth and not have any bumps. Your dog should show no signs of pain when his head is being turned in different directions.

- **LIMBS.** They must be firm and strong, and they shouldn't feel hot to the touch when you run your hands down each limb. Your dog also shouldn't show signs of pain or discomfort. Lift one leg at a time to check if each leg can bear weight.

- **PAWS.** There shouldn't be any blisters or cracks on the pad. Check the dewclaws as well. A dewclaw is an extra nail that hangs on the inside part of the front or hind legs. Make sure it is cut regularly. A hooked, overgrown claw can injure the dog when it becomes an ingrown nail. Paw pads should be exposed for good surface traction; the hair covering the pads should be kept short to prevent your dog from slipping and injuring himself. Long hair covering the pads of his feet makes it difficult for him to walk and makes him more prone to injury.

- **BODY.** It should be free of any lumps, bumps, and wounds. When the dog is viewed from the side, the last rib should be visible under the skin, and when the dog is viewed from the top, he should have a cinched waist. If you can't see his ribs and if he's generally barrel-shaped, your dog might be overweight.

- **GENITALS.** They should be kept clean, should not smell foul, and not have excessive discharge. They should also be free from matted hair or dried fecal matter. Your dog should also be able to pee or poop with ease.

- **OVERALL APPEARANCE.** Your dog should have a shiny and smooth coat. He should also be alert and responsive to your call.

If anything about your dog deviates from this guide, you should visit your vet so you can have your dog checked for any possible problems. Your bi-annual visits will also be much more productive if you share your observations with your vet. You will be able to make sure that your concerns are addressed or you may even play an important role in the early detection of any health issues, preventing permanent injury and potentially saving your dog's life.

Healthcare for Senior Dogs

As your dog grows older, it becomes much more important for you to be attuned to any changes in his body. If humans experience changes or develop diseases as we age, so do dogs, and you need to take steps to keep your senior dog in relatively good condition and to keep him comfortable.

One of your responsibilities is to make sure that your senior dog still gets exercise. At his age, exercise is vital to improve circulation, maintain muscle tone, and prevent obesity. It's a good idea to have your dog walk on surfaces like grass, soil, and sand since they are more shock-absorbent and put less stress on his legs and paws. Swimming is also a good form of exercise for senior dogs, because it helps increase muscular strength without straining the joints and improves lung capacity. If he is new to water, introduce swimming to your dog gradually, and keep an eye on him while he is swimming. Keep in mind that you shouldn't make him swim in deep water right away.

Remember to be mindful and considerate of your old timer's capacity and limitations. Getting him started on an exercise routine should be no problem if he's been getting plenty of exercise throughout his life, but for first-timers, a slow and gradual progression is recommended.

In special cases, you can also bring your dog to animal physical therapists for hydrotherapy, laser therapy, and massage therapy. Therapists and other specialists can help your dog lose weight, ease his aches and pains, or provide appropriate physical

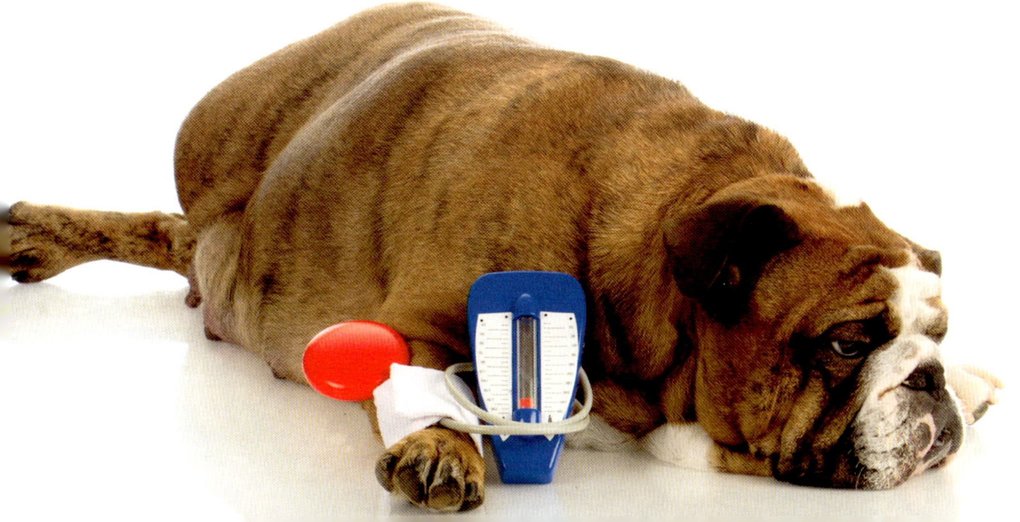

challenges that put the least amount of stress on his aging joints. These therapies may prevent, replace, or at the very least decrease your dog's dependency on pain medications.

For the most part, healthcare for your senior dog is similar to that for an adult dog. Vaccines are still part of his annual routine unless otherwise suggested by your vet. His bi-annual checkup should at least include a comprehensive blood test to evaluate the condition of his major organs. A urinalysis can also check for diabetes and your dog's kidney function. After listening to your dog's breath and heartbeat (auscultation), your vet may recommend an x-ray to examine his heart, spine, or hips, as well as an electrocardiogram to check the condition of his heart.

Common Illnesses Affecting Senior Dogs

As your dog ages, he is bound to face some health issues. Here are some of the most common ones that you can expect.

CONGESTIVE HEART FAILURE. As his body ages, his heart muscles become thinner, weaker, and more relaxed over time. An x-ray will show that the heart looks larger than normal. Its weakening makes it unable to circulate blood efficiently throughout the body.

OBESITY. It's not just a big problem for humans. Obesity is becoming a major health concern for dogs, too. It is caused by excessive calorie intake, improper diet, and decreased activity or lack of exercise. This opens dogs up to the possibility of diseases and complications, such as cardiac and liver problems. The extra weight also speeds up the wear and tear of your dog's bones and joints, and adds pain and pressure to a weak spine.

Obesity in dogs is sequelae of hormonal imbalances. Certain breeds are also predisposed to obesity, such as the English Bulldog, Beagle, Dachshund, Pug, Dalmatian, and Labrador Retriever.

OSTEOARTHRITIS. This is the loss of cartilage on joint surfaces through the normal wear and tear of joints and cartilages. For some dogs, it is caused by predisposing factors like a dysplastic hip or elbow and obesity. Osteoarthritis causes bone callouses to form between the joints due to bone-on-bone contact. When the bones rub together, your dog experiences pain and discomfort, and in advanced cases, lameness.

Early symptoms of osteoarthritis include changes in your dog's gait, decrease in muscle tone and size (atrophy) of the shoulder or hip muscles, difficulty rising from being seated or lying down, and a decrease in his physical activity—your dog might not run, jump, or climb stairs as much as he used to. There may be some changes in his behavior, with your dog becoming either less sociable or more aggressive.

CATARACTS. The lens of the eyes start turning opaque or cloudy, affecting the eyes' ability to focus and the dog's vision.

Cataracts can't be cured or prevented, but early detention and medication can help in preserving vision. They are commonly confused with nuclear sclerosis or the hardening and graying of the lens inside the eye. Unlike cataracts, nuclear sclerosis does not affect a dog's vision and is common in older dogs. It also usually affects both eyes.

It's not only old dogs who may suffer from cataracts. Breeds such as the Cocker Spaniel, Golden Retriever, Poodle, Miniature Schnauzer, and Terriers can develop familial or juvenile cataracts early in life. Dogs with diabetes can also develop cataracts.

SENILITY OR DOG DEMENTIA. When your senior dog gets older, he may start behaving in ways that you've never seen before. These changes are all part of growing old, of course, but dementia will require some extra attention from you. Senility or dog dementia is much like Alzheimer's disease in humans and is caused by a decrease in brain function due to cell death and the accumulation of toxins.

The following are common signs of dementia in your dog:

- erratic and unpredictable sleep patterns
- snaps and growls even when unprovoked, or barks excesively
- doesn't want to be touched and fussed over
- seems lost and disoriented
- no appetite
- unresponsive to coaxing and does not listen to commands
- pees just about anywhere

If you see any of these signs in your old dog, list them all down and inform your vet. He or she can rule out any other medical problem that may be causing these changes. There may be other causes apart from your dog's advanced age. Find out if your vet can recommend medicines that can help deal with these behavioral changes.

- **SPONDYLOSIS.** This is caused by bony projections on the surface of your dog's vertebrae and are also known as bone spurs. They immobilize the spine in that location, and the fusion of the the joints renders the spine less flexible, making it difficult for your dog to move. In some cases, spondylosis also impedes blood flow and pinches the spinal cord and nerves.

Always be on the lookout for the symptoms of any of these diseases, and get in touch with your vet if your dog is behaving oddly or displaying unusual symptoms.

Teaming Up with Your Vet

Refrain from diagnosing and treating your dog on your own. Remember, your vet is one of your most important partners in raising your dog. He or she is the person you can turn to if you are concerned about your pet's health, and your vet can provide all the answers that you need for every stage in your dog's life.

Remember that your vet can address your concerns as a pet owner, but don't expect every single detail to be discussed, especially if you've already reached the point where you're familiar with your dog and the idiosyncracies of his breed. However, you shouldn't hesitate to bring up any additional questions and specific problems.

You and your vet should work hand in hand to ensure your dog's health, which is why you should be open about any changes in your dog, any possible slip-ups you've made, and any incidents which you feel may have affected your dog in some way. Your vet isn't there to judge you, after all, but to help you find the best solution and keep your dog in peak condition.

Make Life Easier for an Arthritic Dog

Here are some ways for you to keep your arthritic dog more comfortable.

- Provide him with soft and supportive bedding. Orthopedic beds are also advisable, and you can also find heated beds that can keep your dog's limbs comfortable.
- Install pet ramps so he wouldn't have to go up any steps. These are good for when your dog needs to get on and off vehicles and furniture.
- Have your dog use elevated feeders and water bowls instead, which can come up to chest height, or place his current bowls on a box or a footstool. These won't require your dog to bend so low to eat and drink.
- If the weather's cooler than usual or you have the air conditioner switched on in your room, your dog should have a warm resting place—the cold can be really punishing on your dog's joints.

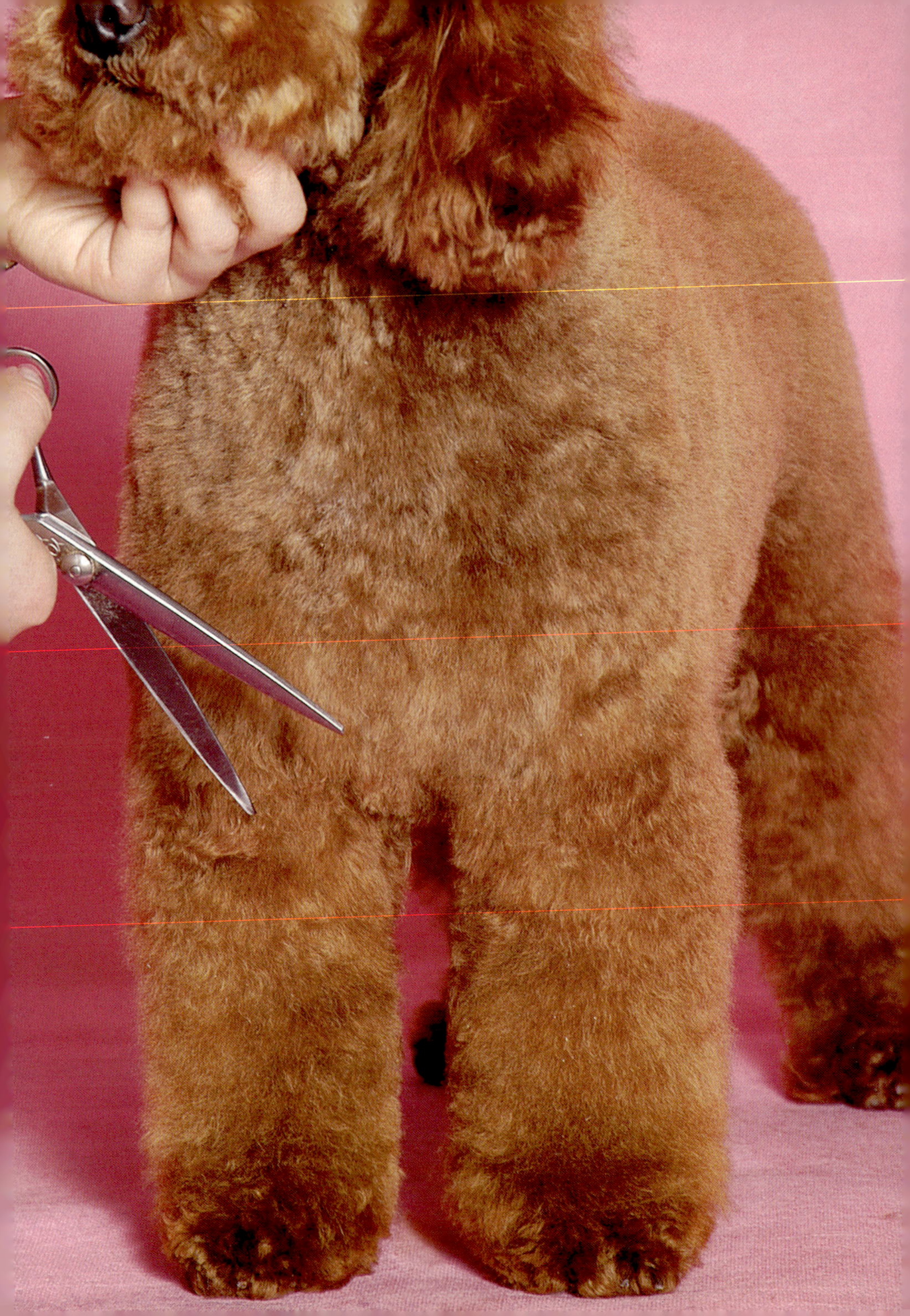

CHAPTER 5

Grooming

Grooming is an important part of keeping your pet healthy. A healthy coat and skin reflects your dog's overall health, and when you do the grooming yourself, you can check him for any bumps, lumps, rashes, or anything else that seems out of the ordinary.

Keeping Your Dog's Coat and Skin in Shape

You should brush your dog's coat every day, whether he is long-haired, short-haired, or has a medium-length coat. This helps minimize shedding and keeps the skin, which is the body's largest organ, in tiptop shape. Brushing not only keeps your dog looking great, but it also protects against external elements, and helps regulate body temperature and retain moisture. Regular brushing also improves the skin's blood circulation and helps your dog's skin get rid of waste and toxins like urea. Use gentle strokes while brushing your dog, taking care to avoid contact with the skin, which can be irritating and uncomfortable for him.

Regular brushing keeps your dog's fur from becoming matted—dematting is painful

for your dog, so try to avoid this as much as possible. Pay close attention to the armpits, thighs, and the area behind the ears, which are all prone to matting. Small tangles can be dealt with using blunt-tipped scissors. Long-haired breeds should be brushed and detangled with a wide-toothed comb.

Cutting and stripping (a process wherein you pull out dead hair using a stripping knife or your fingers) your dog's fur is particularly recommended for long-haired dogs, and optional for short-haired breeds. You can do this on your own or you can take him to a professional groomer.

Basic Bathing Tips

Bathing your dog can be a challenge; some dog owners even joke that it should qualify as an Olympic sport. That's why you should make sure the experience is a good one for your dog. Introduce him to the various items you'll be using—towel, brush, soap, or shampoo—and praise him effusively while he's sniffing them. The same thing applies to the sound of running water. Some dogs tend to panic and hide when they hear water, which they associate with an uncomfortable experience, so let them know that taking a bath is just like playtime—and that there could be a treat or two waiting for him afterward!

You should pick a good spot for bathing your dog. It's generally a good idea to bathe him outside, especially if you have a big dog. But if you don't have enough space, you can bathe him in your bathroom, making sure to line the floor with big plastic sheets or old towels so he doesn't drip all over the place. Warning: You *will* get wet, so wear old, comfortable clothes.

Before his bath, brush and untangle his fur first, removing any visible dirt. It's harder to untangle wet fur.

As a rule, you shouldn't bathe your dog on a daily (or even a weekly) basis. Dogs that live in countries with a temperate climate can do with monthly baths, but because we live in a tropical country, your

dog needs to be bathed once or twice a week. Bathing your dog too often can dry up the natural oils in his skin or coat and cause irritation. If you really want to make sure your pup stays clean in between baths, treat him to a daily brushing instead.

Once you're done bathing him, heap praises on your dog and give him a treat—he's earned it!

Here are the basic steps to giving your dog a bath

1. Prepare warm water, soap or shampoo, and a towel.
2. Wet the dog's body, starting with the back, then moving to the legs, belly, head, neck, and chest. Tuck a cotton ball in each ear to keep water from trickling in.
3. Dilute the shampoo in a small container with water. Pour this on the dog's coat and work into a lather. Scrub the skin well. You can either massage the shampoo in with your hands or use a curry comb or brush.
4. Wet your dog's face and muzzle carefully, avoiding the eye area. Save the face for last to avoid getting drenched since you can expect your dog to shake off the water once you start working on his face.
5. Repeat.
6. Rinse off the lather. Make sure that there aren't any soapy suds remaining on your dog, and check if the dripping water is clear.
7. Towel dry your dog. You can also use a hair dryer to dry him faster. Just make sure you don't point the hair dryer close to the skin and potentially burn your pet. Better yet, use the cold-air setting of the hair dryer.

Brushing Your Dog's Teeth

How often do you brush your dog's teeth? Have you ever thought about doing it at all? If you haven't, you're skipping a very important step in taking care of your pup. Brushing your dog's teeth is often overlooked, even if it's one of the things that can help your dog live a long, healthy life. Loose teeth can really hurt your dog and tooth decay can cause bacteria to thrive in his mouth. Tooth decay also causes renal, cardiac, and hepatic problems once the infection spreads to your dog's organs.

Here are the basic steps to brushing your dog's teeth

1. Prepare the pet toothpaste and toothbrush.
2. Start with the left side. Gently brush the surface of the teeth. Avoid brushing the gums to prevent bleeding.
3. Do this once a day or at least twice a week.

Always make sure that you use toothpaste formulated for dogs; toothpaste for humans isn't good for dogs because it's inedible. You should also steer clear of toothpastes with baking soda, alcohol, and citrus flavors. Vanilla- or chicken-flavored dog toothpastes are much more appealing, and your dog can safely swallow the toothpaste—remember, dogs can't spit out toothpaste like humans can!

Remember to introduce your dog to the whole process first; in the beginning, he won't appreciate having a foreign object and substance shoved in his mouth. Let him examine the toothbrush and toothpaste first, letting him sniff or even take an experimental lick. You may need to have different toothpastes ready to find one that your dog will like.

Begin brushing your dog's teeth slowly. During the first couple of times, you might not be able to get your dog's teeth completely clean, but that's to be expected. Those first few times, your first priority is to make your dog feel comfortable having his mouth touched and his teeth cleaned.

If you won't be brushing your dog's teeth on a daily basis, give him dental toys with ridges and grooved surfaces, as

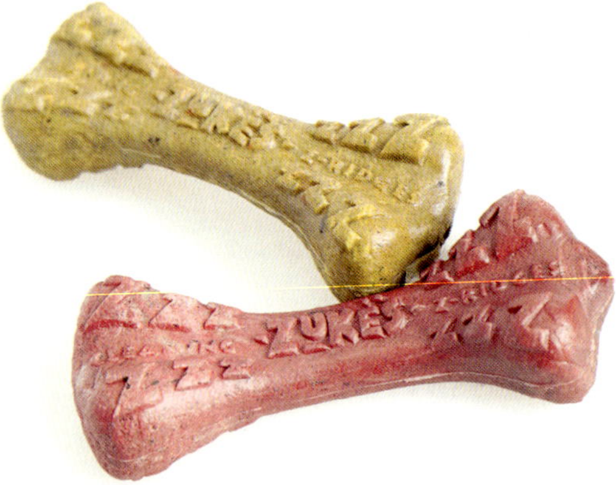

well as hard dog biscuits and treats with enzymes th break down plaque and bacteria buildup to help kee his teeth and gums healthy.

Apart from brushing, don't forget to check you dog's teeth regularly. Look out for any loose teeth or excessive bleeding. These will require professiona cleaning or even dental prophylaxis by your vet.

Brushing the Teeth of an Adult Dog

It's not easy to introduce the concept of brushing to an adult dog, so make sure to train your pet early on. It's easier to get puppies accustomed to having their mouths touched and probed. If you are brushing the teeth of an older dog, a little more care is needed. Start by handling the jaw and lifting the skin of the muzzle gently to expose his teeth. If your dog is fine with this, you can gradually move on to rubbing the teeth and the gums with your fingers or a piece of soft, clean cloth. Don't skimp on the praises—and the occasional treat! Your dog will have a much better time if he receives rewards for good behavior and he will continue to allow you to handle his mouth. This gives you the chance to get started on brushing his teeth.

Cleaning Your Dog's Eyes

Dogs' eyes can be just as sensitive as ours, so they're going to need some care and attention from you. Before cleaning the eyes, check them for inflammation, redness, cloudiness, or dried eye mucus. The presence of excessive eye mucus may be caused by an infection, eye ulcer, or a foreign body in the eye. If you're satisfied that he just has regular, everyday muck that needs to be wiped away, you can proceed to cleaning his eyes.

Here are the basic steps to cleaning your dog's eyes

1. Prepare an eye-cleaning solution. You can also use triple-distilled water.
2. Moisten a clean cotton ball with the solution. Start wiping from the inner canthus (the edge of the eye near the nose or the bridge of the nose). Wipe in a lateral direction, or toward the outer edge, away from the center.
3. Repeat this sweeping motion, taking care not to press on the eyeball.
4. When you're done cleaning one eye, discard the cotton ball you used and use a fresh one to clean the other eye to avoid cross-contamination.

Tear Stains

Tear stains are a big issue for toy breeds with light or white fur, and it's not just because they leave brown or red streaks around the dog's eyes. They are caused by excessive tearing, which may be due to irritation to dust and allergens or a reaction to food. Even blocked tear ducts can cause tear stains. Whatever the reason, cleaning up the stains

or trimming the fur around the eyes isn't an effective long-term solution. Tear stains should be checked by your vet right away because the affected fur can harbor bacteria.

Eye Discharge

One thing you should particularly watch for is a bloody or a yellowish-greenish discharge coming from your dog's eyes. Another red flag is if your dog blinks or tears up frequently. If he exhibits any of these signs, pay your vet a visit. While you're waiting for medical attention, you can also do some first aid on your dog. If you observe him blinking excessively, flush the eye with vet-prescribed saline drops or artificial tears to wash away any foreign objects or any liquids or chemicals that may be present in his eye.

Cleaning Your Dog's Ears

From time to time, you might see your dog trying to paw his ears or scratch something inside. He's actually trying to clean them out. If even he thinks his ears need a good cleaning, it's time for you to step in.

Dogs with pointed ears have it a bit easier than the ones with floppy ears, since their ears can be cleaned easily and dry off more quickly. Dogs with floppy or folded ears, on the other hand, require a bit more attention; there's a bigger chance the ear canal will trap in moisture, making it an ideal breeding ground for bacteria.

Don't put off ear cleaning until it's too late. At worst, your dog might develop an ear infection, which is marked by a heavy discharge with a dark brown or yellow color. Normal ear discharge is simply earwax with a pale yellow or tan color, so you'll know right away if something is wrong when the color is different. Observe your dog's behavior as well. If he tilts his head or scratches his ears a lot and it's accompanied by a pedal reflex, his ears could already be infected. You can also sniff out infection—literally—if the inside of your dog's ear smells bad.

In such cases, you should seek help from your veterinarian right away. It's your vet's job to extract any foreign bodies or parasites such as mites, which are contagious and can cause your dog to produce dark earwax.

Your dog's ears should be cleaned once a week, after bathing, with a specially formulated pet ear cleaner to keep dirt from settling in and to prevent bacteria and ear mites from thriving and potentially causing disease and infections.

Your dog has to be comfortable during the whole process. Some dogs are pretty relaxed throughout the whole procedure, but others can be a little jumpy and refuse to stay still. You can ask someone to help you hold your dog in place or distract him and keep him calm while you're cleaning his ears.

After massaging your dog's ears, cover them with cotton balls so you won't be sprayed with any of the solution and to keep any dirt and earwax from being shaken out of your pooch's ears and onto you or your surroundings.

Here are the basic steps to cleaning your dog's ears

1 Prepare a pet ear cleaner and make sure to read the instructions and ingredients very carefully. Avoid products that contain alcohol, which can cause dryness and irritation.
2 Wet a cotton ball with the ear cleaner. Alternatively, you can flood the ear canal with the solution. To make sure that it fully enters the ear canal, massage the base of your dog's ears.
3 Don't worry if he starts shaking his head at some point. This is actually a good way to shake excess dirt and debris out of his ears.
4 Use a cotton ball to get rid of the remaining solution and wipe off any dirt. You shouldn't dig too deeply into your dog's ears, taking care to reach only the areas that you can.

Flood his ear with the solution.

Massage the base of his ear.

Trimming Your Dog's Nails

It's always fun to hear your dog padding around the house, but you better make sure that there's not too much clattering, because that means you've let your dog's nails grow too long and they're the first things to hit the floor when your dog is walking.

Some dogs are active enough that they're able to wear down their nails. But you need to pay attention if your dog is not very active. His nails could grow so long that they curl in and start hitting the pads of his paws.

Remember to cut your pooch's nails regularly. If you let them grow long, the nail vein grows too long as well. Longer nails are also harder to cut to a length that allows your dog to walk properly. There's also the possibility that long nails could break—ouch!

Here are the basic steps to trimming your dog's nails

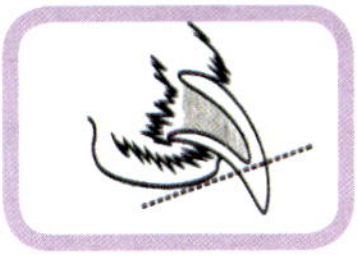
Cut the part of the nail that goes beyond the pad of his paw, 1 cm from the vein.

View of a properly cut nail

1 You need a dog nail cutter and styptic powder.
2 Look at the nail from the side. Hold each nail at its base so it doesn't move around.
3 Cut the part of the nail that goes beyond the pad of his paw. The nails are white, so you can see the tip of the vein inside. Make sure that you cut one centimeter from the vein to keep from hurting your dog.

Allergies, Skin Infections, and Parasites

You need to take care of more than just your dog's coat. Even his skin needs your attention, so look out for any redness, bumps, itchiness, or thickening, as these could be signs of allergy. Dogs can develop allergies to different things, such as their food, dust, fleas, and grooming products. Apart from obvious skin irritation, you can tell that your dog is suffering from allergies if he scratches a lot or constantly paws or licks the itchy areas. His ears might also be red and hot to the touch. In this case, you should check your home for possible causes of allergies—in the air, on the floor, or in something that your dog could've ingested. In some cases, your dog might just be suffering from seasonal allergies. Make sure to take your dog to the vet, so he or she can recommend topical creams, medicated baths, oral antibiotics, or antihistamines.

Parasites such as fleas, ticks, and lice can also plague your dog and cause skin problems, allergies, and serious diseases, so you have to act quickly to get rid of them. If your dog scratches more frequently and intensely than he usually does, it may be time to sit your dog down for a closer look at his fur. Examine his coat and skin carefully while you're brushing him, and take a close look at what comes off his fur. Rub your dog down with paper towels and see if there are any brown stains; these stains come from flea dirt.

Ticks should be dealt with quickly because they could easily embed their heads in your dog and start feeding. The problems ticks cause go well beyond irritation—they could cause serious illnesses. Use tweezers to pull out ticks from your dog's skin, and be sure to protect your hands with gloves. Ticks have to be yanked out directly and every trace of them must be removed.

When your dog is suffering from a flea or lice attack, good, thorough regular baths can help wash away the little critters. Don't forget to clean his bedding, his favorite resting spots, and, while you're at it, the entire house as well, just to make sure that you've gotten rid of the pests as well as their eggs. Your vet can create a treatment plan for your dog as well and recommend any medication that your pet might need.

Fortunately, your dog's skin and coat problems are usually treatable, as long as you get them checked right away. So make sure that you're aware of how much your dog is scratching his skin and that you observe any changes in his coat's condition.

Expressing the Anal Glands

The anal glands, which are two sacs located near the dog's anus, are among the most overlooked parts of the dog. They were pretty useful for dogs' ancestors, who needed to mark their territories with a strong, pungent smell. However, present-day pooches don't really need to do that anymore.

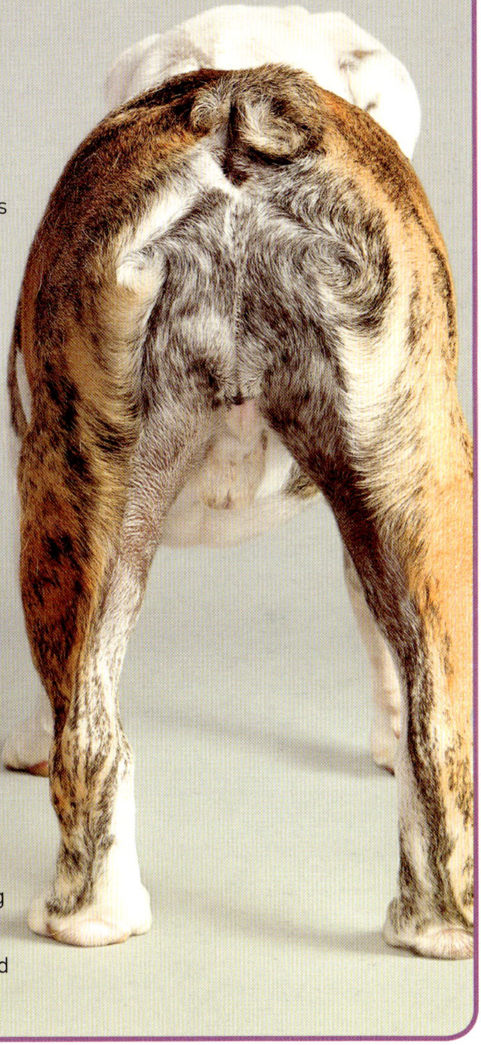

- **For the most part, the fluids from healthy anal glands are drained every time your dog has a bowel movement.** However, a fatty diet and changes in breed morphology tend to cause these glands to become impacted, which keeps them from emptying automatically. If you see your dog dragging his buttocks on the ground or trying to reach his rear, that could mean that his anal glands need to be emptied. Emptying them prevents rupturing, which can hurt your dog or even cause infections.

- **There's really only one way to empty the anal glands: by squeezing out the fluid manually.** You could always have your vet or your groomer teach you how to do this. But if you'd rather not deal with the task (and the stink—the fluid smells unpleasant, to say the least), you can have your vet do it instead.

- **Impacted anal glands shouldn't be something you have to deal with regularly.** Keep an eye on what your dog eats, and ask your vet for help in adding more fiber to your dog's diet, which could help improve his bowel movements.

Grooming Tips for Puppies

Because he's still young, your puppy might not be used to being handled yet. That's why you should make sure he's accustomed to your touch before you start grooming him. If he has a short coat, introduce him to a soft brush at around two months of age, and earlier if he has long hair. At first, your puppy might refuse and try to bite the brush. If your pup is being naughty and trying to bite the brush, you can spray a bit of clove oil or bitter apple on it to discourage him from biting it. You can then use the smooth end of the brush to stroke his entire body, making sure to praise him when he relaxes and lies on his side. Once he's comfortable with this, you can start gently brushing him with the bristles.

Brushing your puppy is an important part of keeping him healthy and well-groomed. When you're brushing your puppy's fur, use steady and gentle strokes and don't brush him too vigorously. Remember that you should brush out the fur and not the skin.

It's tempting to give your puppy a bath just so he gets used to it at a young age, but you must wait for your vet's go-ahead before you start bathing your puppy. A sponge bath can be given starting at the age of two months. Use a clean washcloth soaked in warm water with a little baking soda, which helps neutralize the odor. You can also use dry shampoo formulated for dogs. Clean your puppy's head, mouth, neck, body, and legs. Be sure to wipe the area near your puppy's genitals, where there may be urine burns that appear as red, raised papules or rashes.

As long as you're cleaning your little puppy, you might as well clean the anal area under the tail to get rid of dried feces. Cleaning this area prevents obstipation which gives your puppy a hard time pushing out his feces during bowel movement. You shouldn't just do this every bathtime, but also after meals and after your puppy has a bowel movement.

Remember to choose a bathing spot located away from any drafts and have a thick, dry towel ready to dry off your puppy with after his bath. This will keep him warm and prevent him from shivering.

Most puppies will enjoy early grooming since it's a normal activity for dogs anyway. Mothers tend to constantly lick their pups to keep them clean, mark them with her scent, and stimulate respiration. Grooming your puppy is your way to keep him healthy and shower him with some TLC.

Grooming Tips for Senior Dogs

For the most part, grooming a senior dog works pretty much the same way as grooming an adult dog. However, there are a few special considerations since at your dog's age, there are certain changes in his body that you should take note of.

A senior dog's skin changes with age. It might start looking dry and flaky, or become thinner and more delicate, so you need to be more careful when brushing him. When you brush him at home, you can have your dog lie down to make him more comfortable. If you take him to a groomer, be sure to find one who knows how to handle older dogs and ask for a simple, fuss-free haircut for your dog, one that can be finished quickly so your dog wouldn't have to stand for a long time while he's getting groomed.

Remember to check his skin for any lumps and bumps before brushing. You have to be extra careful that the comb or brush won't snag on these and hurt your dog. Have your vet look at these lumps to find out if they can be treated.

Your senior dog's nails also need your attention, especially because the nails get brittle and harder to cut over time. Because a senior dog isn't as active as a younger dog, he won't be able to wear down his nails with regular walking. You want to keep them at a manageable length that won't affect the way he walks. Trim them every two or three weeks to prevent overgrowth.

It's definitely important to keep your older dog properly groomed, and it's not just to keep him looking good as he ages. It also helps to keep him comfortable and prevents infections and any possible growths from appearing.

Perfectly
Pampered

cloud star®

Say goodbye to Scruffy and hello to Fluffy! Buddy Wash grooming products are specially formulated with natural cosmetic-grade ingredients, including botanical extracts and essential oils for lasting

Products are available in bow&wow®

CHAPTER 6

Socializing Your New Puppy

So much has been written about the importance of socialization and its impact on the future life of a dog. Yet there is no shortage of nervous and fearful dogs that bark, growl, and lunge at people in public. Perhaps because the tasks required to socialize a dog seem simple, many owners believe that socialization is something they can brush off as nothing more than an unnecessary chore. But if you are a dog owner who wants to raise a happy, confident, well-mannered dog that is friendly to all people and other pets in all situations, then socialization is key. Socialization, after all, is smart parenting; it is teaching your dog about the world and how it works. It gives him the confidence and teaches him the social skills he will need to deal with every new and unexpected situation that he will encounter. If you want a dog that behaves like "Lassie," you will have to create it, because such a dog is the product of great parenting skills and requires considerable understanding of socialization.

The Socialization Period

As your puppy grows, he goes through several development periods during which his first experiences will have long-lasting effects. These first experiences, trivial as they may seem to us, will determine, to a great degree, how he will deal with challenges that he will face later on in life.

Probably the most critical of these periods is called the *socialization period*. It begins at around three weeks of age, when the puppy's sense of sight, smell, and hearing have developed and he is now able to move around and explore his new environment. He now becomes aware of the things that exist in his world and begins to establish how he will relate to them.

The socialization period is a short period of time when the puppy will have little fear of the new and unfamiliar, much less than they will have later on as adults. This is the best time to introduce new experiences to the puppy since, during this time, he will recover from potentially frightening situations much faster and with little human intervention.

The Role of the Breeder

Smart breeders will take advantage of this primary stage and will have started exposing the puppies to a variety of stimuli—toys or objects of various shapes, sizes, colors, and textures, as well as all the different household sounds like the television and radio, the vacuum cleaner, and even the hair dryer.

The breeder would also have been wise to introduce human handling at this time so the puppy gets used to being touched and handled by human hands as well as get accustomed to the human scent. This is a time of rapid sensory development; gradually introducing a wide variety of sensory stimuli increases brain activity and development, significantly enhancing the puppy's learning ability. You really *can* raise a smarter puppy!

At five to six weeks old—the second half of the socialization period—the puppy's motor skills are developing and he is now able to move around and explore his environment. During this period, he starts to learn more about the other things in his surroundings and form social attachments to the other beings in his world—both humans and animals.

Through playtime with his dam and littermates he learns the basics of canine social signals and how to use them to get along with other dogs. He learns about dominance/submission relationships from his dam and learns how to play appropriately with others from his littermates. Through play, he also learns how to consciously inhibit the force of his bite so that he doesn't hurt others. He is pretty much learning how to be a dog and how to get along with other dogs. Many breeders fail to see the importance of these life lessons when they separate the puppies from their dam and littermates too early, and end up with puppies with poor canine social skills.

Coming Home

By the time the breeder releases the puppy to his new owner, at seven to eight weeks old, he is ready to learn about the world outside of his litter. As the puppy's new owner, you now take over the dam's teaching responsibilities. You will need to build further on what the breeder has begun and continue with the puppy's socialization. If the breeder has done a good job, you will have an easier and more pleasant time working on your puppy.

The first few days in his new home can be stressful to your puppy. He'll probably feel like his world was suddenly turned upside down. In a very short period of time, everything that was familiar and safe—his dam, his littermates, the smell of the whelping box—is all gone! Thankfully, nature has endowed him with highly developed senses and the right set of instincts to prepare him for this moment. The social lessons he learned from his dam and littermates will have equipped him with everything he needs to make it through this challenge. Your job is to assist him through all these new experiences and make sure that nothing traumatic happens to him.

Bonding

Being social animals, dogs need to bond or carry on relationships with the members of their pack. Without these relationships, the group will not be able to get along. With normal dogs (and normal humans), bonding begins the moment you take your dog home. Each person in the family will have a relationship with the dog. And if there are multiple dogs in the home, each dog will have a distinct relationship with each of you in the family.

It is important to understand that your bond is unique to you and your dog. Bonding happens only when you and your dog are able to focus on each other. It begins with something as simple and mundane as providing for his basic needs—feeding him, taking him out to potty, walking and playing with him, or even just sitting beside him and watching television after a good romp. It is one-on-one time that establishes you as the most important person in your puppy's life—his leader.

As you progress in your relationship, you will learn that you earn your dog's trust and respect by being a reliable provider. He develops steadier nerves because he doesn't have to worry about getting fed, or being left alone during a thunderstorm, or waiting too many hours confined in his crate. He then looks to you to show him what he can and cannot do, how he should and shouldn't behave in any novel situation.

The Fear Period

Toward the last part of the socialization period, there exists a critical period between eight to 11 weeks called the Fear Imprint Period. This is a time in the puppy's development when fears begin to emerge. You will notice an increase in your puppy's apprehension over new things and his fear will surpass his sociability. Anything traumatic that happens to your puppy at this time may have a more lasting effect than if it had occurred at any other time in his life. This could lead to irreversible fears, timidity and/or aggression later on in life. Events like shipping the puppy or having any elective surgery is not advisable at this time. Continue introducing new experiences, but keep everything positive. Guide your puppy gently through any potentially frightening situation.

New People

As he grows up, your puppy will encounter other humans—people of different sizes, ages, and races, people with unique mannerisms, people in uniforms (and hats!) like security guards and nuns, people with loud voices and high-pitched voices (like kids!). All of these can be potentially frightening and can create negative associations about people in general.

Early in the socialization period, introduce your puppy to many different kinds of people so that he does not become fearful or threatened by their presence. Make a conscious effort to figure out what types of people your puppy or dog is not regularly exposed to and set up situations for him to meet these people. If you live alone in a quiet neighborhood with hardly any kids around, for example, you could arrange to have play sessions with kids in a nearby park or in a friend's house. When a dog grows up being fearful and threatened by people, the risk of biting people and strangers also increases. While society will more likely tolerate a dog that is aggressive toward other dogs, it is less likely to accept a dog that is aggressive toward humans.

One way of making your dog associate new people with good things is to have strangers offer him a treat with every encounter. This teaches the puppy to look forward to meeting people as their outstretched hands are a potential source of something good. Also, teaching him to sit quietly for a treat will help him learn to greet people politely and will make him less likely to jump up on them.

Other Dogs and Animals

Throughout his life, you will be bringing your dog with you to many human social situations like dog walks, pet parties, or even simple walks at a pet-friendly mall. Very likely, there will be encounters with other dogs of different breeds and personalities. Your dog must also learn to mingle with them.

Although your puppy has learned the appropriate canine social signals from his littermates, he may not necessarily be confident around other dogs of varying breeds, sizes, and appearances. The other dogs may not even necessarily *look* like dogs to a young puppy. They may have different approaches, expressions, and playing styles and your dog will have to learn to adapt to them.

Again, this can potentially be a distressing situation so be sure to introduce your puppy to new dogs slowly and gradually. Allow some time for the dogs to observe each other from a distance and gain the confidence to approach before allowing either one to come in close for a sniff. If your dog is unsure or reluctant to go near the other dog, respect his feelings and do not force him to go any closer. Allow him to do so on his terms (The same should go for the other dog!). More importantly, introduce him only to dogs that you know to be good and well-behaved. Because dogs learn from each other all the time, you wouldn't want your dog to learn inappropriate behavior from nervous or unsure dogs. Choose your dog's friends wisely!

New Places

Your puppy will also begin to make associations, positive or negative, with particular places. Your home will be his home, his safety zone. Within the home he will also have special places like the kitchen where his food is served, the garden where he will spend many hours with you at play, and the bedroom which he will learn is a place for rest. This is the time you will want your puppy to make associations between activities and the different places of your home so that he knows that playing and running around are only allowed outside in the garden and that the bedroom is a place in which to relax and not for romping.

If you want your puppy to behave appropriately in these particular places, it is your job to also act appropriately and with consistency. In other words, if you do not want him running around inside the house, then you don't ever want to play with him inside the house, especially not in the bedroom.

Alternatively, there will be particular places where the associated activities may not necessarily be pleasant for your puppy, like the vet's clinic where he will see many scared and nervous dogs, or grooming shops with the stressful noises of the dryers, vibrating clippers, and protesting dogs. While it will be difficult, if not impossible, to make your puppy grow a fondness for these particular activities and places, it is possible to teach him to tolerate them by creating more positive (than negative) experiences in these locations.

If you want him to be calm and relaxed at the vet's clinic, take the time to bring him there for short visits even if you don't really have to have anything done. Take him to the clinic, for example, just to get him weighed and then allow the staff or the vets to give him some nice treats before leaving so that he sees that nice things can also happen there, and the people are not always out to hurt him with a needle.

The same goes for grooming salons. Having his nails clipped does not have to be an ordeal. Introduce him to the nail clippers slowly and systematically; create positive associations by feeding him high-value treats the first time he gets his nails trimmed and every time thereafter. The more positive experiences he has at these potentially scary places, the more pleasant your visits will be.

Allowing Him to Recover

Anything new and unfamiliar can be potentially frightening and traumatic. Therefore, it is critical that, when introducing new things to your dog, it is done gradually and always on the dog's terms. If he seems frightened or unsure about anything, do not make a big fuss and simply increase the distance between the dog and the frightening object. Give him some time to recover on his own. The more low-level exposure he has to new things, the faster and easier it will be for him to bounce back from any situation.

Unfortunately, we do not live in a perfect world. Breeders that would have taken great efforts at socialization are few and far between. More often than not, the new owner is left with the bigger share of the work and will have less time to do it because the critical window will start to close at around 12 weeks. After this, the puppy will have a higher tendency to avoid potentially frightening things and more active socialization efforts will be required from you. On the bright side, being with your puppy as he goes through new experiences will strengthen your bond.

The puppy takes confidence in your presence, knowing that you are there to make sure no harm comes to him. So waste no time in taking him out to new places and exposing him to a lot of positive experiences like soccer games and outings at the beach. Let him meet a lot of people, including children, and let them give him treats so he forms positive associations with them. Introduce him to and set up play sessions with a lot of good dogs (and good dogs only, please) so that he learns about other breeds and playing styles. Take him to puppy socialization and obedience classes to teach him English and the rules of the human world. Indulge him in dog sports to help build his motor skills and provide him with lots of physical and mental stimulation. Through all these, your dog will gain the confidence and the social skills he will need to be the darling dog you've always hoped for.

How to Deal with Potentially Frightening Situations

- Expose him to car rides and to passing traffic.
- Walk him on different surfaces—tile, carpet, grass, gravel, sand, cement, chicken wire.
- Each week, have him meet several new people of different sizes, ages, and races, including but not limited to:
  - People wearing uniforms, hats, and helmets
  - Crowds and people clapping, children running, shouting, waving arms, babies crying
  - Kids on bikes, people using canes, walkers, and pushing carts
  - People carrying umbrellas, briefcases, backpacks, and tennis rackets
- Acclimate him to gentle touching and handling and mild restraint by family members and your vet.
- Expose him to common household and yard noises such as vacuum cleaners, lawn mowers, and music.
- Set up regular meetings with dogs, cats, and other animals your dog will routinely encounter.

Safe Socialization

It's important that exposure to all these new and novel experiences is kept safe, positive, and stress-free for your dog. Here are some guidelines:

- **Until the puppy has had a full set of vaccinations, set up play sessions in a safe environment.** Many well-meaning vets will tell you not to bring your new puppy out because of the risk of contracting an illness. However, the truth is that more dogs die today not from disease but from behavior issues due to a lack of socialization. So while there is a small risk that your puppy may be exposed to illness while socializing with other dogs, you can further minimize the risk by setting up socialization sessions in safe environments and with dogs you know. Set up play sessions in your friends' houses and disinfect if needed. Carrying him instead of letting him walk when you take him to public places lets him take in all the sights and sounds without the germs. There is no excuse not to socialize your pup!
- **Use common sense and be in control of all situations so you can keep it positive.** Avoid situations, people, and environments that you think might result in a less-than-happy experience for your puppy. Choose only well-behaved kids (and adults) and dogs for your puppy to meet. If needed, tell people how to behave around your new puppy.
- **When introducing anything new, let the puppy approach on his own.** Give him the opportunity to investigate and let him take his time.
- **Respect your puppy's feelings.** Never push or force your puppy if he's at all reluctant. Let him recover on his own.
- **When something does frighten your puppy, don't make a big fuss about it.** Let him see that it's not a big deal for you and calmly take him out of the situation.
- **Keep it fun!** Maintaining a calm and positive attitude toward the things that may frighten your dog will help him get over it faster.

CHAPTER 7

Training

For some reason, a lot of people, when they bring a dog home, expect him to figure everything out for himself. But the truth is, things like doing his business in the right place or walking obediently without pulling on his leash are behaviors that do not come naturally to a dog.

Although there are dogs that figure things out for themselves even without formal training, they are exceptions to the rule. More likely, you will end up with a dog likes to chew on shoes, run around the furniture, jump on guests, and pee all over the house—in other words, one that behaves like a typical dog. Nine times out of ten, you end up with a normal dog and all you need to do is invest time and effort in training him before (and not after) things start going wrong and the once-cute puppy grows into a nuisance.

Rarely are there any "problem dogs" in a litter of puppies other than those with inborn health issues. Problems occur when dogs become victims of circumstance, mismatched with the wrong owners, like a Labrador Retriever with a 70-something couple who is under the impression that they make great family dogs. Somehow they missed the part saying that Labs also happen to be very active hunting dogs!

In the majority of cases, however, dogs become problematic because they are forced to live in a human environment without any structure and where they are not taught how they are expected to act. This is what training is all about. As it is with socializing your dog, training is about being a good dog parent and putting order in the life of your dog. It's a job that you will want to—and should—do yourself.

Dog training is the same. Fortunately, there are now local dog training classes where they teach the fundamental concepts of how dogs learn and how to build a better relationship with the use of positive training methods. Attending these classes is highly recommended.

Where to Start

With the wealth of training information available today, you might think it's easy enough to learn how to train a dog by simply getting a book or looking up information on the Internet. Then again, the amount of information available out there can be overwhelming. There are so many training methods—new ones, old ones, even "trainer-to-the-stars" methods that are more often than not in conflict with each other, leaving you (and consequently your dog) more confused than ever. As with all the information published on the Internet, you will need to exercise caution and obtain information only from sites published **by legitimate and qualified professionals.**

It also helps to remember that training your dog is a mechanical skill, much like riding a bicycle. If you are a beginner, you can't really become proficient in it by reading a book or watching videos. You would have to ask someone who knows how to ride a bike to teach you how to do it.

You would then need to actually get on a bicycle, start pedaling, and fall over a few times until you learn the concept of balance.

Reward-based Training

Among all the current training methods available, more and more people are discovering how much easier it is to use positive, reward-based techniques to train their dogs. These people have learned that training is not so much about forcing your will upon your dog, nor is it about teaching him circus tricks (although you could!).

Training is more about teaching your dog to understand English so that when you bring him into a novel human situation—when you are having guests over for a dinner party, for example—you will be able to communicate to him how he is expected to behave. It's teaching him not to jump up on the guests or to grab food from the buffet table. Because unless a dog is taught how he is to behave in any and all human situations, he will only behave as all dogs know how to behave—like a dog!

By consistently rewarding only desirable behaviors and ignoring the undesirable ones, a dog quickly learns which behaviors are valuable and will benefit him the most. As a result, these behaviors are more often repeated while the ones that don't result in anything lose their value and are ultimately discarded. Training thus becomes a game—a fun, engaging activity where the dog is an active and willing participant and his human, an awesome game show host who doles out amazing prizes (i.e., rewards)!

Rewards

Think of rewards as currency that you pay your dog for performing good behaviors. Keep in mind that even among humans, when you get paid for doing something, you are more willing to do it and to do it over and over again. The higher the value of the currency, the harder you are willing to work for it.

The same is true for dogs. **Rewarding a behavior reinforces it, and *not rewarding* it extinguishes it.** For some dogs, the currency with the most value is food treats like slivers of chicken. For other dogs, the preferred currency is a ball or tug toy. And still for others, it's attention and petting. If you are to be an effective trainer, you must know which particular currency or currencies he will work hard for.

Life Skills

The most important lessons you will be teaching your dog are the ones that involve self-control—restraining himself from what his dog instincts compel him to do. In many real-life situations, dogs are subjected to stimuli that trigger his basic drives, like when his owner comes home or when food is placed on a table. The temptation to jump up for attention or grab that food is just too much for a dog.

But with great patience, training, and understanding, plus the trust you have built into your relationship, you will actually be able to get your dog to go against his instincts and choose the more appropriate behavior. When he does, you must praise and reward him lavishly.

Trainer's Tips

- **For most training applications, food treats are a good choice for rewards. All dogs enjoy food, and treats are quick to dispense and consume so that you can do a lot of quick repetitions during a session. When introducing a new skill or a difficult one, use a high-value food like slivers of roast chicken or little bits of boiled liver—whatever it is that makes your dog go bananas.**

- **Cut them up into little bits no bigger than an M&M (even smaller for tiny dogs!) so they don't get full. Dog biscuits don't do well as training treats as they take too long to chew. You can make a "trail mix" of assorted bits of food so the dog doesn't tire of the food reward quickly. When using food as a reward, train just before meals so that your dog is hungry and will be more interested in what you have to offer.**

Getting Started With Training

Here are a few basic skills you should teach your dog. There are many ways to do this. This are just one of the few ways that work.

skill no. 1 Attention: Teaching a Dog His Name

One of the first things you will want to teach your dog is to pay attention. Many dog trainers will tell you that attention is everything. If your dog isn't paying attention to you, then you will have a more difficult time asking him to do anything else! It is also a good way to start teaching him his name, which is going to be your cue for him not just to look at you, but to come to where you are and give you his full attention. It's a really simple but very powerful exercise.

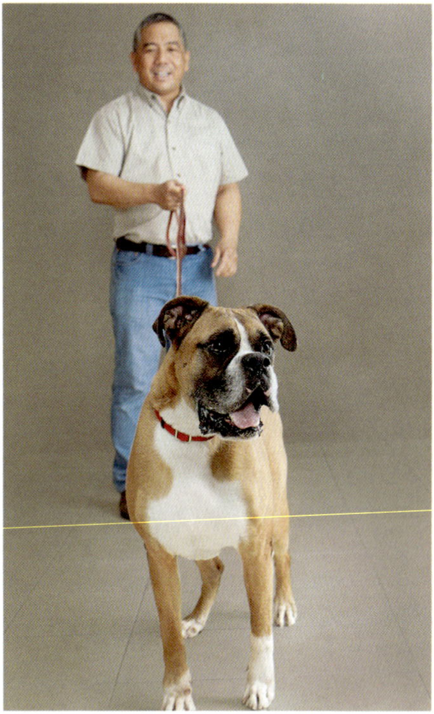

1. **Choose a quiet environment (preferably indoors, with no distractions) and stand in the middle of the room with your dog on the floor in front of you. Make sure you have a bunch of treats in your pocket so you can quickly reward your dog at the proper time.**
2. **Your dog will probably be wondering what you are doing and what he is expected to do. He will also probably be interested in the treats you have in your pocket. Ignore him for a while, but watch him from the corner of your eye. When he starts to realize that nothing much is happening, he will start to look around the room for something more interesting.**
3. **The moment he starts to walk away from you, call his name ONCE in a nice, happy tone, as if you have something exciting for him (you actually do!). When he turns around to look at you, say, "Yes!" and quickly take out a treat from your pocket and hold it by your leg to lure him back to you. Give him the treat when he comes to get it.**
4. **After giving him a treat, ignore him again and repeat the exercise about five to 10 times. As with all training exercises, you want to end when the dog is still asking for more so that when you do another training session later, the dog is going to be an even more eager student.**

Tip: Don't worry if your dog doesn't respond to his name immediately. He needs some time to associate his name with the act of coming to you. If you call his name once and he doesn't respond, try making kissing noises or clapping your hands to get him to come to you instead of repeatedly calling his name.

Once the dog is responding to his name, you can then progress to walking around the room and having him follow you around. Call his name and reward him for following. As you walk around the room, there will be things that may catch his attention. Call him back the moment he starts to walk away and reward him for choosing to come back and pay attention to you instead of the distractions around the room.

Teaching a Dog to Relax

- One of the first life skills a puppy or a new dog must learn is relaxation. Surprisingly, some dogs do not know how to relax. In some energetic breeds, calmness actually has to be taught because it doesn't come naturally. Most of the time, a dog grows up becoming excitable simply because he learns it early in puppyhood when humans squeal and get all excited around him. (How can you not?) Very quickly he learns that being excitable, jumping up, and mouthing or licking is how he is supposed to behave because it is what gets him attention. So when teaching your dog to relax, keep in mind that you must first be relaxed yourself whenever you are around your dog. Any excitability that you show will almost always get him in an aroused state.
- One of the easiest ways to teach your dog to relax is to catch him while he is already in a relaxed state. The best time is usually after he has been running around or just before naptime. When you catch your dog lying around or just sitting calmly, nonchalantly give him a treat. The first few times that you do this, he may come out of the relaxation and start to focus on you for the food. Simply ignore him (nonchalantly, of course) and wait till he's back to being calm and relaxed. Wait until he is not looking at you before you give him a treat again. If he doesn't relax right away, leave him and try the exercise again later. Reinforcing your dog whenever he is calm will teach him to choose calm behaviors and actually enjoy it.

skill no. 2

Sit

"Sit" is probably the most commonly taught skill to dogs as it is among the more useful. Asking your dog to sit keeps him still and prevents him from getting into all sorts of trouble. Also, a sitting dog cannot jump on people.

1. In a quiet room with no distractions, stand with your dog in front of you and without saying anything, hold a treat to his nose.
2. Slowly raise the treat straight up, about a foot high above his nose. This should make him raise his nose to follow the treat and cause him to drop his rear into a "sit."
3. The moment his rear touches the floor, give him the treat, making sure he keeps the sitting position. If he raises his rear as you give the treat, quickly withdraw the treat and lure him back into a sitting position. Only when he is sitting properly do you release the treat.
4. After he gets the treat and before he starts to get out of the sitting position, say, "Okay!" and move a couple of steps to the side to let your dog know that he can now get out of the "sit" position. "Okay" will now be your release cue from the "sit" position.
5. Repeat this several times until your dog learns that putting his rear to the floor is what gets you to release the treat. You will know this when your dog willingly offers the "sit" even before you put the treat to his nose.
6. Once your dog is offering the behavior on his own, you no longer have to lure him into a "sit." You can now add the verbal cue "Sit!" and continue to reward him every time he gives the correct behavior. By doing the exercise in quick succession, your dog will learn to associate the command with the behavior.
7. After a few sessions, ask your dog to sit with your hands on your side and the treat out of sight, hidden in your pocket. If he goes into a "sit," quickly take the treat out of your pocket and reward the dog. This tells you that your dog now understands the word "Sit."
8. Once your dog is reliably sitting when you say the word, work at different times and locations. Ask other people to say the command and reward your dog whenever he gets it right. Consider saying the command in a nice, happy voice rather than a deep authoritative tone. This makes your dog a more enthusiastic participant in the training process.

skill no. 3

Down

Like "Sit", "Down" is also taught to keep the dog still and out of trouble. It is a more relaxed position than "Sit" and therefore can be held by the dog for a longer period.

1. **With your dog standing in front of you, hold a treat to his nose and SLOWLY lower it in a straight line to the point on the floor between his front paws.**
2. **As your dog follows the treat to the floor between his paws, he will have to go into a "bow," placing his elbows on the floor. Keep holding the treat in that position, allowing your dog to nibble the whole time.**
3. **After a while, your dog will tire of being in the "bow" position and find it more comfortable to lower his rear to the floor in the full "down" position. When this happens, release the treat and praise him. Say, "Okay!" and ask the dog to get back up and repeat the exercise several times. As with the "Sit" command, you will use a release word like "Okay!" to tell the dog he can get out of the "down" position.**
4. **After a few sessions, your dog will know what you want him to do and will start to go into the "down" as soon as you hold the treat to his nose. This is the only time that you start to introduce the command "Down." Say it every time you put the treat to your dog's nose.**
5. **As soon as your dog starts to offer the "down" position on his own, little by little you will no longer need to put the treat to his nose and lure him down. Work to simply say the word "Down" and when he goes into the "down" position, reward him promptly.**

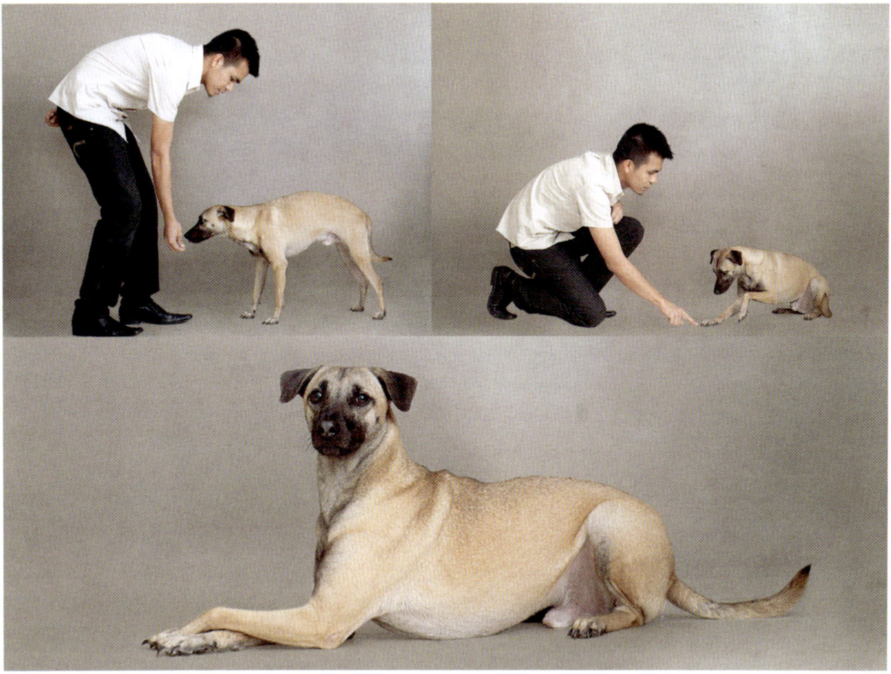

CHAPTER 8

Exercise and Play

When you bring a dog into a human home, you must understand that you are asking him to live in an artificial, if not an alien, environment. Living in a human home, the dog is deprived of all the sensory stimulation he would otherwise receive outdoors. The stress and anxiety that builds up from the deprivation will have to find an outlet somewhere and if not, will result in anxiety-related behaviors. Chewing on shoes, jumping up on people, and running around the house are just some of the ways that dogs will try to get physical and mental stimulation and relieve themselves of stress. So in order to coexist peacefully with humans in a home environment, dogs need to get a considerable amount of exercise and play in their daily routine.

In the wild, predatory animals like wolves and wild dogs naturally get their exercise from chasing after fleeing animals, pouncing on them, and wrestling them to the ground. Even during play, their behavior patterns are the same, switching between the roles of predator and prey. Your dog is the same. In order to provide him with the physical and mental stimulation he needs, you will have to engage him in an activity that appeals to his prey drives. If you have a pure breed dog, it becomes easier when you know what particular job your dog was bred to do. A Labrador Retriever, for example, would find great satisfaction in a game of fetch, where he gets to run after a ball and carry it back to you, especially when he has to swim to get it. On the other hand, chasing a squeaky toy and tearing it to pieces will be a liberating experience for a Jack Russell Terrier. The type and duration of exercise will vary with every dog.

Walking or Running

Probably the simplest way for your dog to get some exercise is by taking him out for long walks. Walking your dog (apart from the five-minute potty breaks) allows him to explore the world outside and enables him to experience many outdoor scents, sights, and sounds. Generally, a 30- to 45-minute walk twice a day should be good for most dogs. With younger or more athletic dogs, or highly active breeds, a lengthier jog or run with lots of stops in between may be necessary to fulfill his exercise needs. New dogs and puppies will have to be taught how to walk on a leash without pulling on it. For obvious reasons, it is so much easier to teach a puppy than to correct an older dog that has had a lot of experience dragging people around.

Before walking a young puppy, however, you must make sure that his vaccinations are complete. Very young puppies can pick up potentially fatal diseases from the streets, so you will want to keep him safe. Practice walking him indoors first or in other safe places that are not open to feral animals. Learning to walk on a loose leash is essential if you plan to run with your dog. When you start to run, it triggers your dog's instinct to run and pull ahead of you. Until you have taught your dog to walk without pulling, do not try to run with him. Once your dog learns to walk beside you, then you can start increasing your pace, slowing down or stopping whenever your dog starts to forge ahead.

Teach Your Dog to Walk on a Leash

Because of their highly developed senses, dogs will always be distracted whenever you take them outdoors. All the different sights, scents, and sounds are just begging to be explored! This is such a big part of being a dog and it is also the biggest challenge when walking your dog.

- When people take their dogs out on a leash for the first time, the dog's initial impulse is to rush up to whatever catches his attention. Instinctively, people pull back on the leash and here is where the problem begins. Pulling your dog on a leash creates what's called an opposite reflex and makes your dog pull even more. Pretty soon, you and your dog find yourselves engaged in a pulling match. So the first thing to do when walking your dog is to never pull your dog on the leash and always keep the leash relaxed.

- Instead of pulling your dog, teach him to follow you by rewarding him with treats or praise whenever he walks along with you. Reward him also when he looks up and pays attention to you while walking. This encourages your dog to follow you rather than pull on the leash.

- When he gets distracted by something else in the environment and starts to pull on the leash, stop and call him to you. When he responds by coming back to you, reward him again with treats or praise, further encouraging him to walk along with you and AWAY from the distraction.

- Remember that your treat rewards must be something of high value to your dog. Biscuits may not be enough especially when you are walking outdoors. When using praise, you must do so with a lot of enthusiasm and excitement to show your dog how pleased you are.

- Start this exercise only when your dog or puppy has gotten used to the collar and leash. Practice indoors at first where the distraction levels are low, and slowly progress to the outdoors when you are more successful at calling your dog and keeping his attention on you.

Toys

Most dog toys available in the market today are designed to appeal to a dog's predatory instincts and get him to run, jump, grab, tug, and even to tear or chew! Balls, Frisbees, squeaky toys, tug toys, chew toys—these are among the best-selling toys because dogs LOVE them.

Using toys as part of a dog's exercise is mentally stimulating and can be a great stress reliever for both owner and dog. Many dog owners, however, complain that their dog will be interested in a new toy for all of five minutes, 10 at the most, if it hasn't been torn to pieces by then or if the dog hasn't gotten bored and moved on to doing something else. Desperate to keep their dogs preoccupied for longer periods, hapless owners can fall into a vicious cycle of buying toys at every opportunity to keep their dogs calm and out of trouble.

Well-meaning owners need to realize that the fun of playing with toys does not come from the toy itself. The fun comes from the interaction with another individual playing with the dog. Of course, there is no better playmate for your dog than YOU. Remember that the toy is only a tool used to enhance the game and nothing more. Many are surprised to learn that even an old rag or an empty plastic bottle can become the most fascinating toy in the world in the hands of a really great primate, er, playmate.

Canine Disc Play

More popularly known as canine frisbee, canine disc play is a simple yet highly stimulating activity for energetic dogs. It taps into their desire to chase, jump, grab, and retrieve a fast moving object. Although not all dogs will immediately take to catching a flying disc, they can get quite addicted to it once they understand the game. Canine disc play only requires that you are able to do a decent disc throw, and the dog does the rest of the work. It's great for healthy, highly charged dogs that need more than a daily walk!

Dog Agility

If running or playing fetch with your dog still leaves him wanting more, you may want to consider the sport of dog agility. It's basically an obstacle course for dogs where the dog has to run through a course of hurdles, tunnels, weave poles, and contact obstacles in the shortest possible time. Speed, accuracy, and attention to the handler are the skills required of a dog, so you will need to enroll in classes or join an agility club for lessons in order to participate in this sport. The rush is extremely rewarding for both owner and dog!

Swimming

If you live near a body of water or have access to a pool, swimming is another activity that dogs will take to very quickly. Breeds like Retrievers and Poodles are natural water dogs and will spend hours jumping in and out of the water. Some dogs will immediately take to the water with no problem while others will need some coaxing before jumping in. What's important is to introduce your dog to the water gradually, perhaps with a baby pool, before taking him to a much larger body of water. Swimming is a low-impact exercise and is great even for senior dogs and therapeutic for those with physical disabilities.

Fun Nosework

Fun nosework is the pet version of substance detection training where a dog is taught the finer points of using his nose. It is a fairly young sport developed by detection dog trainers in the United States looking for other ways to enrich the lives of pet dogs. Instead of teaching the dog to search for contraband like drugs or explosives, pet dogs are taught to find essential oils. Though not as physically demanding, a session of nosework can tire a dog out as much as, if not more than, a long walk. It is a mentally demanding activity that can be fun for practically any breed of dog. Because the dog works independently and one at a time, nosework works well for dogs that do not get along with other dogs.

Trick Training

Teaching your dog to do tricks is more than just for impressing your friends with his skills. It's more about challenging your dog to perform beyond his existing abilities. Because he is an animal capable of complex thinking and behavior, getting your dog to do things like getting a can of soda from the refrigerator builds his confidence and opens his mind to doing more than what a dog would ordinarily do.

Humans tend to view work and play as two separate and distinct activities. To a dog, they are one and the same. No matter what breed of dog you have, you need to provide activities that will enrich your dogs life. A life without exercise and play is a life without fun. A life without fun is no life at all.

CHAPTER 9

Travel

These days, you see people hanging out in parks with their pets, dogs walking on a leash in shopping malls, and even small dogs being carried around in supermarkets. It's a really positive change from the days when dogs were simply not allowed to go anywhere, with their owners being turned away due to concerns that the dogs they have in tow might mess up a place or get rowdy.

But you can't just leave your dog alone at home, especially if there's no one to look after him for the day. Plus, taking your dog out is an essential step in the socialization process: Meeting different people and other dogs ensures that he will learn how to behave around others and helps your dog become more accustomed to being in new places and situations. You also want to take every opportunity you can to bond with your dog, apart from the time you spend playing with him at home.

If you're planning to step out with your dog, there are a number of things that you should keep in mind to make the experience a great one for you and your pup. First of all, you should make sure your dog is safe; keep him in a well-ventilated and sturdy carrier or dog bag when you're driving or commuting. This is more comfortable, not to mention safer, for you and your dog than if you keep him on your lap while driving, give him free reign to move about the vehicle, or keep him tied up using his leash. Additionally, if you're taking a cab, it's a good idea to have your dog in a carrier out of consideration for people who aren't comfortable around dogs. During walks, keep your dog on a leash—remember that this is mandated by city ordinances.

Aside from a dog carrier and leash, you have to keep the following items handy when you take your dog out, whether you're commuting or simply out and about with your dog in a park.

- **Water.** If you think it gets uncomfortably hot during the day, imagine how much warmer your dog feels, especially with all that fur. Giving him water from time to time keeps him cool and hydrated. Be sure to take him out on bathroom breaks, too.
- **Wet wipes.** Clean up your dog with these in case he runs into something dirty on the street.
- **Plastic bags.** You need these to clean up after your dog after he does his business. Places that welcome dogs usually have plastic bag dispensers, but it's always wise to have your own supply just in case.
- **A leash with collar.** Have this ready so you can walk your dog and let him stretch his legs.
- **Treats.** Having a handful of treats can satisfy your pup's belly while the two of you are out and there's not enough time to give him a proper meal.

At present, there aren't any laws that focus on the issue of allowing pets onboard public transportation, so the matter still depends on the preferences of the operator of the vehicle. Some cab, bus, or jeepney drivers may agree to transport you and your pet, although it would be best to ask for permission first. Keep in mind that pets are prohibited on the MRT-2 and the MRT-3.

Going on Car Trips with Your Dog

When planning a car trip with your dog, the most important thing to keep in mind is that it's dangerous to leave your dog in the car, even if you roll down the windows and the weather outside is cool. Your dog could suffer from heatstroke or suffocate.

If you're thinking about going somewhere with your pet, check that the places where you are headed—and your stops—are pet-friendly. A bit more thought should go into planning longer road trips with your dog. For starters, you need to make sure that your dog will be fine during the trip. Car rides, even short ones, can be stressful for dogs who aren't used to riding cars, aren't brought outside often enough, or associate car rides with trips to the vet. The prospect of visiting the vet

tends to cause anxiety in most dogs, and if his car rides so far have mostly taken him to the vet, expect him to behave anxiously even if you're heading to a different destination. To avoid this problem, make sure to occasionally take him to places that he loves, like the park or a house where he gets lots of attention and playtime. You can even give him a treat after the ride.

Dogs are capable of making associations, and they are able to pick up on the fact that car rides can take them someplace fun. Here are some preparations you should make for your road trip with your dog.

- Take a look at the route you'll be taking for the trip. Schedule stops every one or two hours so you can take your dog out for a quick walk and potty break.
- Contact your vet and get advice on what your dog may need during the trip.
- Get information on any veterinarians in your destination, just to make sure that you know who to get in touch with in case of an emergency. Prepare your dog's medical records so the vet can provide your dog with the appropriate treatment. Establishments where you might need to go in case of an emergency might request that you present your dog's records and health certificate.
- To prevent nausea, have your dog fast for six to eight hours prior to trips that will take longer than six hours. Just make sure to give him water when he needs it. Fasting is not necessary for trips that are shorter than six hours.
- Place an identification collar on your pet. This is a safety measure in case he wanders off and gets lost. You may also want to include the address and contact number of the place where you will be staying.

Be Sure to Pack the Following Items to Ensure Your Dog's Comfort

- Familiar items, like your dog's favorite toys. Bringing them on the trip can make your dog feel that he's in a safe place.
- A food bowl and a water bowl.
- Enough dog food and treats for the entire trip plus a little extra just in case. Once you're at your destination, stick to your dog's feeding schedule. If he's used to eating at 11 a.m., that's the time you should give him his meal during the trip. Feeding him commercial dog food is ideal in this case since it's easier to pack and serve.
- A pet carrier to keep your dog safe in any situation, such as during a boat ride, when you have to leave him in an area that is not secure (like the hotel lobby), or if your dog is not yet potty-trained and you need to leave him in the hotel room.
- If he's used to using a bed, bring the bed on the trip. Your dog needs something comfortable to sleep on, and something that smells familiar will help put him at ease.
- Your dog's brush and comb. You need these for grooming your dog during the trip. These can help keep him clean especially since there may not be enough time or the right facilities for bathing him.
- If your destination has enough room for you to give your dog a bath, bring soap or shampoo as well in case he gets into a wet or sticky situation.
- Medications and a first aid kit (see Chapter 13 for tips on what you should put in your dog's first aid kit).
- A towel for rubbing your dog clean after a particularly energetic play session.

Health Problems Your Dog Might Encounter During the Trip

When you're stepping out with your dog, you want it to be be a fun experience for both of you: You get to run errands or see a different place and unwind with your best buddy, and he gets to see the world, sniff out new spots, and win some new admirers and playmates.

But it may not be fun and games all the time because your dog could actually develop health issues while on the road. One of the things you should be observing is how much your dog is eating while you're in a new place or while you're on one of your rest stops. A dog who's a regular traveler should be fine, but one venturing out for the first time might experience the following:

Lack of Appetite

In certain cases, inappetence is a cause for concern, but in this situation, it is just a sign that your dog is experiencing some anxiety and stress over the unfamiliar surroundings and activities. But if your dog is a travel veteran, this should not pose a problem. He will sleep during the entire trip, pee and potty during pit stops, and enjoy exploring a new place.

This can also happen when you move to a new house and your dog is still getting accustomed to it. As long as your dog is still active, you don't have anything to worry about. Your dog may miss a meal or two, but he should go back to his usual feeding habits once he's settled in and comfortable in the new place.

Constipation

The whole experience of being in a new place or the trip itself may also cause constipation in dogs. This doesn't have anything to do with whatever he ate—it's mainly stress that's making him constipated. When this happens, make sure he drinks plenty of water and add rice bran or psyllium husk to his food. See to it that he gets enough exercise as well. Exercise helps boost your dog's metabolism, regulates his system, and promotes bowel movement.

Nausea

Nausea or motion sickness is another problem you might have to deal with during car trips with your dog. Puppies are especially susceptible to this, since their ear structures, which also help with balance, aren't fully developed yet. Even older dogs can suffer from motion sickness if they haven't been able to outgrow it. Vomiting is a sure-fire sign that the car ride is making your dog feel carsick, but you can prevent vomiting by watching for certain signs: excessive salivation, whining, shallow breathing, and inactivity.

If your dog is prone to motion sickness, you should make sure that he's as comfortable as possible during a car ride. Make sure that he sits facing forward; a dog harness can help keep him in place (and safe in case of an accident). You can also have him fast at least six hours before travel or feed him half his usual serving of food. You can help your dog overcome his motion sickness by getting him used to car rides prior to your trip. Take him on short, 10-minute drives before your scheduled trip, increasing the travel time as your departure date approaches.

Lastly, don't forget to maintain a cool temperature inside the vehicle, as this can help make your dog feel more comfortable.

Irritation

Dogs who don't suffer from carsickness seem to find joy in sticking their heads out the window and letting the wind blow in their faces. However, this can cause eye irritation, since dust or debris could fly into their eyes. Make sure that you have saline eye drops at hand to rinse out your dog's eye in case of redness, itchiness, and irritation. Be reminded however that this practice isn't safe. He could get hit by oncoming traffic or jump out the car window. It would be safer to just roll down the window a little bit to let fresh air in, but not so much that he can stick his head out the window.

While you're at your destination, you should also watch for any skin irritations that your dog might develop. Rashes and insect bites could appear while your dog is off exploring, rolling around in strange areas, or playing in saltwater. Use tonic or alkali water to rinse off your dog's body to neutralize any irritations, and apply an ice pack on the red or swollen area for 10 to 15 minutes, two to three times a day. Don't forget to bring a first-aid cream with antibiotic, antifungal, and anti-itch properties for insect bites or other types of skin irritation. See a vet if your dog's symptoms persist.

Don't let the possibility of illnesses stop you from taking your dog out though. Your pup will enjoy exploring a new spot in the city or maybe even an entirely different province where he can run to his heart's content or splash around on the beach. You simply have to make sure that you're prepared for any possible ailments your dog might develop. Keep all these guidelines in mind and you'll be sure to have a fun day out with your dog, whether you're traveling within the city or out of town!

Flying with Your Dog

Pet travel policies and requirements vary depending on the airline and the country. They change from time to time. So if you are flying with your dog, we recommend that you contact the airline of your choice and the embassy of the country you are traveling to (for foreign travel), and consult with your vet in order to learn the exact steps you need to take and all the requirements you need to fulfill. Local and foreign air travel will have different policies and requirements.

Bringing Your Dog to the Beach

Keep these guidelines in mind if you're planning to take your dog to the beach.

- Find out if dogs are allowed on the beach where you're going and ask about their house rules.
- Your dog may think that the beach is one giant litterbox; have poop bags ready so you can pick up after him.
- Bring water for your dog. You want to keep him hydrated, given the combination of his high energy and the heat of the sun.
- Keep an eye on your dog. You want to be sure that he'll be well-behaved. Also, even if he knows how to swim, you shouldn't let him go into the water without supervision.
- Bring his favorite toy, a ball, or a Frisbee. A game of fetch by the seaside will really invigorate your dog.
- Wash off saltwater after his swim to avoid irritation and drying. Have a thick towel ready to dry your dog off or rub the sand off his fur at the end of the day.
- Do not bring him out when it's too hot. He may hurt the pads of his paws or worse, suffer heatstroke!

CHAPTER 10

Common Behavior Problems

Dogs will be dogs and they will behave in ways that will not necessarily fit your idea of how they should carry on in your household. Running and jumping around, chewing, barking, and digging are NORMAL dog behaviors but would be considered inappropriate in the human home. When owners fail to recognize the need to teach their dogs the appropriate behaviors, dogs will default to their natural behaviors and make a nuisance of themselves.

Nuisance behaviors, more often than not, are *learned* behaviors that dogs have acquired on their own because engaging in them has brought about favorable results. Jumping up, for example, is something they do naturally as puppies to get their mom's attention. When they try this on their humans, the common reaction is to pet and *give* attention to the cute puppy. Inadvertently then, the owner has rewarded the puppy with attention for jumping up on people. And because it has been rewarded, the puppy then grows up repeating the behavior which constantly gets reinforced. This is tolerable and cute while they are still puppies, but when they grow up into 80-pound dogs, it's not going to be so cute anymore. *When nuisance behaviors present themselves, it is useful to try and look at what it is that the dog is seeking and what is reinforcing or feeding the behavior. Simply removing the reward will often diminish if not extinguish the behavior.*

Jumping Up

As mentioned above, jumping up is a very natural behavior that puppies and dogs engage in when greeting people, especially when their owners come home at the end of a long day. Because they are either tired from the stresses of the day or excited to see their beloved pet, owners often like to make a big fuss when their dogs rush to greet them at the door, petting lavishly and arousing the dog's excitement with animated dialogue. The dog learns very quickly that this is the behavior expected of him when owners or other humans come in through the front door. Even when owners try to discourage this behavior later on by shouting, "No! No! No!" and pushing the dog away, he sees that as a reward for this behavior, since he is still greeted with a lot of fuss.

Teach your dog that calm, relaxed behavior is the appropriate greeting behavior at all times. In order to do this, you need to be calm yourself whenever you enter your home. Only when your dog is calm and relaxed and not trying to seek your attention do you call him and initiate greeting. If your dog jumps on you, *do not say anything.* Just turn away and back off to avoid getting jumped on. Do not make eye contact as this can also be perceived by your dog as attention. Stand still and wait for him to calm down, with all four feet on the floor, before giving him any attention. If he starts up again, simply withdraw attention and again wait for relaxed behavior. This process can take as long as five or 10 minutes before the dog is able to relax, so just be patient and wait it out. If you are dealing with a particularly strong, pushy, 90-pound dog that has been rewarded for jumping on people, it may be necessary to keep him in a room before you enter the house and let him relax in there before you initiate any contact. It's one of those things that gets worse before it gets better. What's important is for you to be consistent.

Hyperactivity

All dogs enjoy intense physical activity and many of them will actually seek it from puppyhood all the way to maturity, at which time (if they were raised properly) they will begin to calm down. This is probably why many new pet owners complain that they have a hyperactive dog. The truth is, truly hyperactive dogs are relatively rare. A true hyperactive dog is one that is unable to relax even after you have given him plenty of attention, exercise, and mental stimulation—only a veterinary behaviorist can confirm a diagnosis.

Certain breeds have a greater need for activity and exercise than others, particularly those that were bred for work, like herding dogs, hunting dogs, and Terriers. These dogs are happiest when doing a particular "job," and do not cope well with inactivity when left alone for long periods. If you have one of these breeds and your dog has resorted to redecorating your living room, he may not be getting enough physical and mental stimulation. Find out what your dog was bred to do and give him something that will

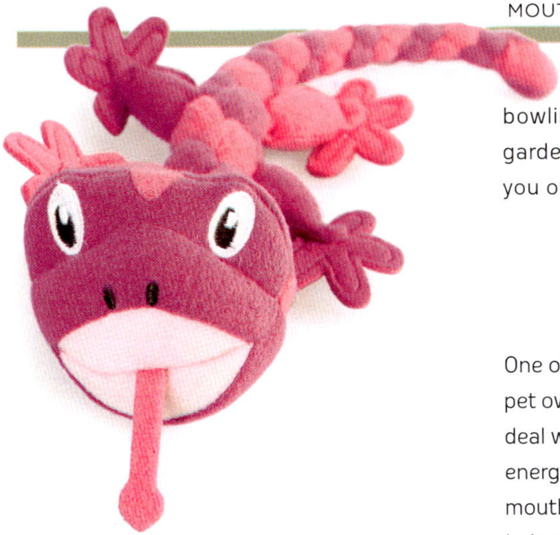

substitute for that activity on a regular basis. Border Collies are highly intelligent dogs bred to "think" on their own, so they will do well with a challenging sport like dog agility. Hunting dogs like Pointers and Labrador Retrievers can be kept satisfied by throwing a ball into a swimming pool and letting them fetch it over and over again.

Working dogs are natural athletes and can work hard physically for long hours at a time so a 30-minute walk or run may not be enough to satisfy him. You will be wise to tire him out mentally. Engage him in mental activities like scent work by hiding treats all over the house and having him look for them. Teach him fun and complex tricks apart from the basic obedience exercises. If you are a nine-to-five person, make use of interactive toys and puzzles that keep the dog busy and engage his mind. One Jack Russell Terrier named Harry de-husks two coconuts as part of his daily regimen. When none fall from the tree, his owner gives him a 12-pound bowling ball that he rolls around in the garden for hours. Creativity is a must when you own a highly active dog.

Mouthing, Nipping, and Play Biting

One of the most common complaints of new pet owners, mouthing can be a challenge to deal with especially with pushy and highly energetic dogs. From puppyhood, dogs will mouth, nip, and play bite as part of their social behavior, usually to initiate interaction or play. When highly aroused during play, things can get out of hand and the force of the play bite often causes injury to human playmates.

As puppies, dogs learn to inhibit their bites during their first couple of months with their littermates. During playtime, they practice fighting and learn how strong they can bite before it starts to hurt their playmates. However, some puppies never get to learn these important life lessons when they are separated too early from their litter by the breeder, or when they are the lone puppy in the litter. With these puppies, the responsibility of teaching bite inhibition then falls on their humans and should be taught as early as possible.

When a puppy starts to mouth or play bite, owners can try yelping just as another dog would when at the receiving end of the play bite. This usually surprises the puppy, and a couple of repetitions should be enough to teach him to soften his bite. With a more pushy or energetic puppy, it may be necessary to stop all play and interaction and walk away to teach the dog that the fun stops when he starts to play bite.

In most cases, mouthing and play biting are unknowingly reinforced by the owners themselves. Many times, when an owner is playing with the puppy and the puppy starts to mouth, the usual human reaction is to repeatedly say, "No, no, no!" while pushing the puppy away. To the puppy, this reaction appears like the human is excited by the play biting so he gets more aroused and does it even more. Instead of discouraging the behavior, the human ends up reinforcing it and making it more fun for the puppy.

It must also be noted that some puppies and dogs actually do not enjoy being touched around the head and neck area, while some humans, on the other hand, can't seem to keep their hands off of their dogs. Putting your hands and touching the puppy can trigger mouthing and nipping, especially in some northern breeds like Chow Chows and Siberian Huskies, so it is important that owners recognize this in their dogs and respect it.

To discourage mouthing and play biting, it is best to keep your hands away from the puppy's head and neck area and use an appropriate toy that the puppy can bite on instead of your hands. Keep the attention of the puppy on the toy and make it interesting to play with by shaking it and making it "come alive." Using a ball or squeaky toy that you can throw away from you gets the puppy off of you when he starts to go for your hands or clothes.

Sometimes when a puppy or a dog is mouthing, he is trying to communicate something to you and mouthing is one of the few ways he knows to get your attention. A dog may mouth to say he needs to go potty or to let you know he is hungry or thirsty. A puppy or dog will also mouth to get you to play with him, but consider first that there may be some basic need he is asking to be met.

Destructive Chewing

Dogs don't have hands like humans do, so they explore their world using their mouths. Whenever something interesting catches their attention, they will interact with it by sniffing, licking, pawing, and yes, putting it in their mouths and chewing. This is part of their nature and it is one of the ways they get stimulation from their environment. The usual targets are shoes, remote controls, electrical cords, and the legs of furniture. Hence, when we bring a dog into our home, we need to dog-proof the areas of the house that are accessible to the dog. If there are things of value that you don't want chewed up, keep them out of your dog's reach. Remember that

anything at knee-level and below is fair game. Close the doors to parts of the house that you don't want your dog to explore. Be smart.

Sometimes, long periods of separation from their owners can cause great anxiety in dogs, especially when it comes right after a short period of intense play and interaction. For example, a newly acquired dog that is brought home on a weekend and gets lavished with so much attention and play from its humans will, come Monday morning, when the humans all disappear to go to work and he is left alone all day, become stressed out and seek relief by chewing on various household items.

Instead of punishing and reprimanding your dog, it is better to redirect him to more appropriate chew toys. Natural bully sticks are great as are edible chews when you need to leave him alone for a while. Rawhide, especially the artificial ones, should be avoided as these are not very healthy for dogs and present a choking hazard.

The best way to deal with destructive chewing is similar to how you deal with hyperactivity—provide your dog with enough exercise and stimulation on a daily basis. Avoid leaving him alone for extended periods of time and put him on a regular schedule so that his day becomes very predictable and does not cause anxiety. Challenge him by feeding him from one of those interactive toys that you fill with kibble so that he has to figure out how to get at the food inside. This burns off excess energy as he chases the ball—and his meal—around the yard. Keeping your dog's mind active eliminates the need for him to look for stimulation elsewhere.

Nuisance Barking

Barking is generally accepted as normal dog behavior, but when it becomes incessant or when it happens in the early morning hours, it can become irritating for the owners and their neighbors.

Dogs will bark for a variety of reasons. The most common is when it is triggered by something frightening, threatening, or something he wants to get at like the newspaper delivery guy, a cat, or another dog. This is exacerbated when the dog is in a cage, kept behind a fence, or tied by the gate. Over time, the barking can get reinforced whenever the target of the barking goes away: Your dog makes a connection that his barking makes the frightening thing go away. For this reason, it is not advisable to keep dogs by the gate where he is unsupervised for long periods of time and is always in full view of passersby.

Dogs that are kept in cages or outdoor kennels all day may also bark for attention. The need to go potty outside the cage or perhaps to simply get relief from the heat can be expressed through barking. Being social animals, dogs do not thrive on being left alone outdoors. The need for companionship and the boredom that comes from being alone causes them to bark for someone to come. And when someone does come, the barking gets rewarded as the dog learns that it works. Interestingly in some cases, dogs can become fascinated by the sound of their own bark and will carry on all day for lack of anything else to stimulate them.

The solutions to nuisance barking are as varied as what causes it. But it all boils down to only two ways to stop it and to prevent it:

- **Remove the trigger.** Keep the dog away from the gate where it has a view of anything and everything that it will bark at. Caging a dog or tying a dog out by the gate does not offer much of a security advantage anyway—CCTV cameras and motion sensors will do a better job and are much cheaper to maintain.

- **Supervise the dog.** These days, a companion dog's proper place is indoors with his humans. The only time that he is brought outdoors is whenever he is being played with, exercised, or trained. Living with a dog requires that you provide him with training and sufficient enriching activities to prevent any anxiety-related behaviors like barking.

Digging

Digging issues are most common among Terriers or "earth dogs," dogs that were bred to hunt rodents by digging through their underground tunnels. These dogs find great fulfillment whenever they are covered in dirt. Other breeds like Beagles, however, will also dig for buried "treasure" or bury toys and treats to keep other dogs from finding them. Labradors will dig under hedges to make a cooler place to lie in.

For these dogs, the simplest solution is management. You either fence in your flowerbeds or supervise the dogs whenever they are in the garden. One of the more practical solutions to the problem is to give your dog his own sandbox and hide his bones or favorite toys in it for him to dig out. By making the sandbox more interesting than your hedges, you are hoping that your dog will ignore the latter. Even then, he would still need to be supervised whenever he is outdoors.

House Soiling

Even among toilet-trained dogs, there will be some that are prone to house soiling—peeing or pooping inappropriately inside the house even though their frustrated owners have done everything to prevent it. There can be an underlying medical issue and pet owners must try to identify it in order to address the problem. Bladder and other urinary infections are definite suspects as well as urinary incontinence or polyuria. In these cases, the vet is your best bet.

Dogs that are bought from pet shops are especially prone to house soiling, having spent entire days or more in their cages. These dogs have learned to potty in their living areas due to the abnormal living conditions in which they were forced to exist. Unlike normally raised dogs, these dogs have lost the aversion to their pee and poop. Some would have even learned to play with them, or worse, consume them out of sheer boredom. These can be some of the most difficult cases to solve with normal toilet-training methods. These cases will require a strictly controlled diet and additives like S.E.P. (Stop Eating Poop) as well as close supervision.

Incomplete or inconsistent toilet training can also lead to house soiling. Some good breeders would have started toilet training their puppies and new owners are delighted to see that the puppies will automatically go on paper. Just because a puppy is already going on paper does not mean that he is already toilet trained. New owners must pick up where the breeder left off and continue the puppy's training as he adjusts to the new home environment.

Anxiety is also a common cause of house soiling. This can be due to social issues like when an individual or dog leaves the home, or when a new one becomes part of the household. New objects like a baby carriage or luggage introduced into the home or a new dog that comes over for a visit can also trigger urine marking. It is best to consult a behavior specialist in these cases.

Prevention

Great dog owners will recognize that the best way to solve nuisance behaviors is to prevent them from taking hold in the first place. It is so much easier and takes less time. The behavior issues outlined above make it apparent that most of these undesirable behaviors develop when the dog's needs for regular exercise and mental stimulation are not sufficiently met. As early as possible in a dog's life, and as soon as you bring the dog into your home, introduce him to the rules of the house—train him—to give him a sense of structure and hold him accountable to what you teach. We cherish our dogs for all the wonderful things they bring to our lives but bad habits don't need to be part of the package.

CHAPTER 11

Sexual Maturity And Breeding

There are a lot of major changes that you will need to deal with when your dog reaches sexual maturity. On average, male dogs achieve sexual maturity at the age of six months. For female dogs, smaller breeds achieve sexual maturity as early as six months, while larger breeds go through it when they're one year or older.

A dog who's sexually mature exhibits certain physical and behavioral changes. Not all dogs exhibit all the signs, but you might observe a few of them in your dog. A male dog might start marking his territory, lifting his leg and peeing in small amounts on different corners or areas. He might also start acting more aggressively toward other dogs, and have a stronger tendency to escape and roam around. Mounting, either as act of dominance, to assert himself, or signal sexual interest, is also another sign.

A female dog, however, will begin going into heat, characterized by a swollen vulva, enlarged nipples, and the presence of bloody discharge. She might even start humping other dogs, and begin to raise her behind and move her tail out of the way—a behavior known as "flagging."

When Your Female Dog Is In Heat

Your dog's heat cycle has four phases: proestrus, which lasts for seven to 10 days, wherein your dog will start bleeding; estrus, wherein your dog will welcome male dogs for mating; diestrus which, if the dog is pregnant, will last for two months or until the puppies are born. If not, diestrus becomes part of anestrus, the last phase, which is the period of rest until the next estrus. Female dogs usually go into heat up to four times a year, so you have to watch for the signs and be ready every time.

You also have to be prepared for some changes in your female dog's personality during this time—believe it or not, she's going to have some mood swings. She can become more hotheaded, start losing her appetite, or be more sleepy. For other dogs, a common condition called pseudopregnancy or false pregnancy can also occur. She might actually start eating more, vomiting, experience weight gain and swelling or engorgement of teats due to milk production. Your dog might also exhibit nesting or aggressive behavior, wherein she may get overly protective of a toy or any small object. Her body thinks she's pregnant, and her behavior is simply being influenced by maternal hormones.

Remember that behavioral changes in your dog around this time aren't anything to worry about, bacause they're fueled by hormonal changes. However, while some actions can't be totally prevented due to hormones, a well-trained and properly socialized dog will have more discipline and restraint, so it's always advisable to train your dog well and have a good relationship with her.

Spaying and Neutering

Puppies are little bundles of cuteness. However, while they're definitely a lovely addition to your home and family, taking care of puppies and raising them can be hard, especially when you're unprepared to house them and you're unable to find people who are willing to adopt them.

Since raising a large litter takes far more time, effort, and money than one is usually able to spare, some people end up giving the puppies away or abandoning them. You could give away the first litter to friends who will really love and take care of the puppies, but you may find it difficult finding good homes for the succeeding litters. Letting your dog have lots and lots of puppies doesn't mean that you're an animal lover. You certainly shouldn't let your dog have puppies just because you think it will be cute to have them around the house and that it would be a great experience for your dog to be a parent.

As a responsible pet owner, you should also make sure that you actively contribute to helping control the problem of animal overpopulation. Just consider the fact that there are already more than enough stray dogs roaming the streets, unwanted and homeless dogs, and dogs in shelters just waiting to be adopted.

If you find that you're not prepared to look after both your adult dog and a new set of puppies, you might want to consider having your dog spayed or neutered. Spaying (which is for females) and neutering (which is for males), also known as "fixing," are performed to prevent your dog from reproducing, thus ensuring that you wouldn't have to deal with an unwanted litter or have puppies who will not get the right amount of attention and care that they need. Raising puppies takes a lot of work and you have to make sure that you can give both your adult dogs and the puppies the time, attention, and the resources they need to thrive.

Some people think that simply keeping their dogs indoors or having them wear a diaper or underwear can prevent them from reproducing. These don't always work, because you can't keep your dog indoors all the time and dog diapers or underwear isn't always an effective deterrent. Getting your dog fixed is the only way to guarantee that he won't reproduce.

Some specialists recommend having the procedure done before your dog reaches sexual maturity. Dogs can undergo the procedure when they reach six to 10 months

old, depending on the breed size. In males, the testicles normally descend by the third month. If the testicles or a testicle does not descend, it becomes all the more important to remove them. Undescended testicles, usually located in the inguinal area or inside the abdomen, are prone to developing into tumors and should be surgically removed.

Spaying involves opening up the female dog's abdomen and completely removing her uterine horns, ovaries, and adjacent ovarian tissue. Spaying offers a number of benefits apart from preventing unplanned pregnancies. For starters, it lowers your dog's risk of developing breast, uterine, and ovarian cancer. This also keeps her safe from developing pyometra or pyometritis, which is an infection wherein pus accumulates in the uterus. Any inconveniences and risks associated with heat cycles and mating will also be avoided. Getting your female dog spayed can also keep male dogs away and stop them from "stalking" or mounting her. A good time to get your dog spayed is before or after she first goes into heat, or when she is approximately eight to 10 months of age.

Neutering the male dog, on the other hand, involves removing the testicles, and should be done when he's approximately six to eight months of age for small to medium breeds, and at around 10 months to a year for giant-sized breeds. It completely eliminates the chances of developing testicular cancer and reduces the risk of prostate infections. It can also keep your dog from jumping and mounting, as well as stops or lessens territorial marking. Plus, neutering lowers your dog's aggression levels and reduces his desire to escape or roam. You have to remember, however, that there is no guarantee that such behavior will stop; your dog's personality plays a large part on how he behaves. It does not depend solely on whether he's fixed or intact.

If you are going to have your dog spayed or neutered, you should find a competent veterinary surgeon who has performed these procedures before. You can ask your regular vet for references if he or she doesn't do these surgeries. The veterinary surgeon will be able to answer any questions or ease apprehensions you might have, as well as let you know how to minimize or eliminate the risks or complications involved. He or she can also give you advice on how to ensure your dog's speedy recovery.

What To Expect Post-surgery

Spaying and neutering are considered major surgeries, so it's completely understandable if you're nervous about getting your dog fixed. Don't worry, though—your dog will be under general anesthesia so he won't feel a thing throughout the process. Once he comes out of anesthesia, however, he's going to be pretty drowsy and will spend a good deal of time sleeping after the surgery. Make sure to help him when he's climbing stairs or generally walking around, since his balance won't be at its best. Don't expect him to be energetic and playful yet—your dog shouldn't move around so much because of the stitches. You also have to clean and disinfect the incisions every day.

Apart from a lower energy level, your dog's appetite may also be affected. Don't force him to eat. Just prepare a small amount of food to keep him nourished.

Overall, you should just let your dog relax and recover after the surgery. He should be up and about after a few days, and any unusual changes should be reported to your vet right away. Ask your veterinary surgeon for post-operative care instructions so you know what else to expect and how to attend to your newly fixed dog's needs.

Some Myths About Fixing

There are a number of myths about spaying and neutering that may have influenced your decision on whether to have your pet fixed, which is why it's important to read up on facts that dispel these myths.

MYTH 1: Fixing makes your dog fat.
Your dog's weight depends solely on his exercise level and how much food he eats.

MYTH 2: Your dog will be upset about losing his reproductive capabilities.
Your dog won't be worrying about whether or not he is capable of having children.

MYTH 3: Female dogs need to experience being a mother.
You need to remember that dogs aren't like humans. While dogs will exhibit maternal behavior to their puppies or even to other creatures, it still isn't an indication that motherhood is their priority.

MYTH 4: It's expensive to get your dog fixed.
The Philippine Animal Welfare Society (PAWS) offers veterinary services, including spaying and neutering. Spaying female dogs costs P1,500, and neutering male dogs costs P1,000. For both males and females, you have to pay an additional P500 for every 10 kilograms in excess of 15 kilograms. They also have a spay-neuter program for pets of indigent families.

MYTH 5: You should let your dog have a litter first before spaying.
Certain cancers are more easily avoided if you spay your dog before she achieves sexual maturity or gives birth.

Other Options

If you're not having your dog spayed or neutered, there are injectible contraceptives available for male dogs, and female dogs can take either injectible or oral contraceptives. However, these are not available locally and you will need to import them. Furthermore, these contraceptives have some side effects that could affect your dog's health, such as liver damage, infertility, increased risk of vaginal infection and indoor wetting, body odor, skin problems, vaginal distortion, personality and behavior changes, uterine infections, mammarian cancer, breast enlargement, and weight gain.

Because these contraceptives offer no guarantees and there are a lot of complications and risks involved, your best option is still to have your dog spayed or neutered.

Conscientious Breeding

As early as when people begin to think about acquiring their first dog, they will already be considering the possibility of breeding. Knowingly or unknowingly, it has already been a part of the decision-making process. “Do we get a male or a female?” or “Perhaps we ought to get a pair!” At this point, people will hardly think about the number of dogs in need of homes at local shelters, nor the number of dogs that are being given up before they reach their first birthday. There is no available statistics in the Philippines, but the number of abandonment cases being called in daily to the Philippine Animal Welfare Society is a clear indication that the number is growing.

The point being made here is not about breeding dogs but about *breeding without thinking.* People will breed their dog for frivolous reasons, from wanting to have cute little puppies running around the house to wanting to teach their child about the miracle of birth. The biggest offenders, however, are those that breed entirely for profit. These people breed indiscriminately, by the dozen of every popular breed, and with no regard for the quality of the puppies they are producing. This type of breeding has spawned an entire culture of commercialism that produces “teacup” or undersized dogs, dogs with heart, skin, and respiratory problems, as well as dogs with serious temperament issues, not to mention a lot of duped owners that now have to spend for medical bills and behavior classes just to be able to live with these dogs. It is clear that the new pet buyers and owners need to start making the right choices.

Before we even consider breeding our dogs, there are a few points that will need some serious consideration.

Keep in mind that the dog we have is a product of others before us who cared enough to pair the right stud to the right bitch and took charge of the birth of every single generation. We must honor the love and devotion that went behind the breed with which we are working today by keeping it pure, strong, and correct.

We have an obligation to study and learn all about the breed to know what is correct about its appearance, movement, and temperament before we even tamper with it. So much information is available today from books, magazines, and the Internet. There is no excuse for ignorance.

Breed only dogs that are of excellent quality and know what you have. You need to be able to evaluate your dog objectively to see its strengths and its weaknesses against the breed's standards. If we must breed, we must breed for excellence, with the sole purpose of improving the breed. Poor genes need not be propagated.

Regardless of specific breed traits, a dog that is being considered for breeding must be in excellent health and free from any genetic defects. His temperament, above all, must be excellent. We cannot let ourselves be fooled into thinking that because the dog has a good head, his fearful disposition is excusable.

Probably the most serious consideration is your commitment to the puppies you will produce. Breeding is both time-consuming and expensive. You will need to do some soul searching before you proceed. Ask yourself these questions:

- **Do I have the time to devote to the puppies until they are old enough to go to their new homes?**
- **Do I know enough to advise new owners on the proper rearing of the puppies—their diets, training, and potential health issues?**
- **Will I be able to afford the health tests such as hip x-rays for OFA certification and other health tests prior to breeding? And in the case of a Caesarian operation, will I be able to afford it?**
- **Do I know enough about a dog's reproductive process? Do I know enough about whelping? Do I know enough about raising healthy puppies and socializing them?**
- **Will I be able to place all the puppies in good homes?**
- **Should anything happen in the lives of the new owners, will I be able to take back the puppies or re-home them?**

Unless you can answer yes to ALL of these questions, you should consider neutering or spaying your dog instead. It will help to know that there is no shortage of dog breeders. If you would like to add another puppy to your brood, it is much more convenient to acquire one than to breed one yourself.

CHAPTER 12

The Homestretch

Your dog has been an important part of your life for so many years now that it's hard to imagine your house and your life without him. Even if you knew that this day would eventually come, it's never easy when it does, and you can never truly prepare yourself for the loss of your dog. The only thing you can do is to acknowledge that your dog's time will indeed come, that it will be difficult for you when it does, and that you should still be there nevertheless for your dog until the very last moment.

Euthanasia

Choosing to put your dog to sleep has got to be the most difficult decision a dog owner could ever make. Should the time come, you need to be ready and look at every single aspect of the matter to determine whether or not euthanasia is indeed the best thing for him. On one hand, you want to hang on to him for as long as you can, and not say goodbye if you really don't have to yet. On the other hand, you can see that he's already in pain, but you don't think you can take the responsibility of being the one to choose to end his life. You really have to think long and hard about this choice, consult your family who also love your dog dearly, and observe your dog's health and behavior to determine whether you are indeed acting in his best interest. Your vet can also help shape your decision, since he or she understands the health issues your dog could be going through.

You should also ask yourself the following questions: Can he still eat and drink on his own? Does he refuse food? Is he mobile, and can you still take him on those walks that he loved so much? Is he still curious and playful? Does your dog still show a zest for life? If the answer to most of these questions is "no," then it's reasonable to conclude that your dog's quality of life has been compromised.

Don't forget to consider how healthy your dog is, or if he is already suffering from some painful and debilitating illness or condition, greatly reducing his ability to enjoy life. If your dog seems comfortable enough and doesn't appear troubled or in pain, you may choose for him to pass on naturally. However, if your pet is suffering from some terminal disease and has no chance of recovery, if he has been undergoing treatment for some time and hasn't shown any improvement at all, or if he is restless and having difficulty doing the simplest things, like breathing, then perhaps it's time to put him to sleep.

You may also be concerned about your finances and the costs of keeping your dog alive. Don't be ashamed if this thought has crossed your mind. Being practical is not a bad thing, and if you've exhausted all the options to keep your dog in good condition, there is no possible way for you to ever be considered a bad dog owner. Your dog is also a part of your family, and the last thing he would want is for you to put yourself in a difficult situation.

Believe it or not, even your vet may find it a difficult and emotional experience to perform euthanasia, even if it is the humane and sensible thing to do. It is never easy to end a dog's life, especially one with whom the vet has built up a connection over the years. For you, the dog owner, deciding to put your dog to sleep and having to say goodbye to him is doubly painful. You can, however, take comfort in the fact that your friend is no longer suffering.

What to Expect During Euthanasia

Once you've decided to have your dog euthanized, it helps to prepare yourself for the process. Your vet will require you to sign a consent form, which will contain your information and your dog's details, and indicate that you fully understand the procedure and the reason for it. You can choose to have it done in your vet's clinic, although you can also have the procedure done at home. The latter could be a better option since this means that your dog will be in a comfortable, familiar environment. If you're taking him to the vet, you should also decide whether you want to be alone or if you need a friend or a family member to be there with you.

Remember to stay calm. Your dog might pick up on your tension and nervousness, and may become agitated.

The whole process, from beginning to end, lasts less than 10 minutes. First, your vet gives your dog a sedative to keep him calm. It will only take a single needle prick to sedate him if your dog doesn't already have an intravenous catheter. For the second and final injection, your dog will be given an overdose of the euthanasia solution, which will make his heart stop. Your dog will then pass away peacefully.

Your dog will basically be asleep during the process and he won't feel a thing once the barbiturate takes effect. So there's no need for you to worry about putting him in more pain than he was in when he was alive.

What to Do with Your Dog's Things

Throughout his life, your dog received a bunch of great toys. Some of them may not have survived for more than a week, thanks to his enthusiastic playing. Others may be well-worn. Toys that are still in good shape can be washed or cleaned and donated, or passed on to a younger dog. Don't hesitate to throw away those that are really old and tattered. However, you might want to keep one or two toys that your dog really loved that will always remind you of him.

When Your Dog Dies of Natural Causes

You may decide to bring him to a veterinarian for a *necropsy*—the body will be opened up, similar to autopsies that are conducted on people. Each organ is inspected to see if the probable cause of death can be identified. Remember to take your dog to the vet immediately; the body must not be more than six hours old. There are, however, limitations to the investigative work that can be done, such as toxicology, due to the lack of local facilities and its high cost.

Dog Burial Options

Your dog gave you such joy when he was alive that it only seems right to give him a proper resting place. Fortunately, there are now options for pet owners who want to lay their dogs to rest with the respect that they deserve.

You can choose to either bury your dog or have him cremated. For a commercial burial, your dog will be picked up at the vet's clinic or your home, and he will be buried in a marked or unmarked grave. The choice will depend on you, as well as on your budget. If your dog is being cremated, he can be picked up at either the vet's or your home, and his ashes will be placed in an urn, which may be made of marble, stone, or wood. The urn will then be returned to you. It all depends on the pet burial service you will be choosing.

Here are companies/groups that offer pet burial services:

Noah's Ark Pet Columbarium

http://www.noahsarkpetco.com

This pet memorial park and columbarium is located in The Garden of St. Michael the Archangel, Pascual Compound, Sucat, Parañaque City. Noah's Ark also teamed up with Paradizoo to create the first pet columbary in the Philippines.

Pet Valley Park and Crematory

http://www.facebook.com/petcremationphillippines

Located in Silang, Cavite, Pet Valley offers burial and cremation services. Their packages include paw printing and hair sampling.

Philippine Animal Welfare Society

http://www.paws.org.ph

While PAWS no longer accepts pets for burial, the group welcomes donations to put up a plaque for your pet, which can feature your pet's picture and a short dedication, on their Pet Memorial Wall.

Rainbow Bridge Pet Aftercare Services

http://www.facebook.com/rainbowbridge.ph

Rainbow Bridge is based in Quezon City and accepts pets from all over the country.

Their packages include cremation and a personalized urn. Fees depend on the weight of your dog.

Vets in Practice

Dr. Nielsen Donato offers pet cremation services, although burials are accepted as well. The lot is located in Pansol, Laguna.

If you have plenty of room in your backyard, you might also want to consider designating a small spot in the garden for your dog. You can find out if a casket can be made for your dog or you can also opt to wrap your dog in a shroud before burying him. A common practice is to have your dog cremated and bury the ashes in your garden after they have been returned to you. You could also put up a marker on the exact spot where you buried him and even have a small ceremony for your dog.

The Grieving Process

You should allow yourself time to grieve and not think that it is unusual for you to feel the way you do. Losing a pet is a hard thing to deal with, and the memories will be sure to have an effect on you.

You have every right to feel sad and hurt during this time, and there's no need for you to try to appear strong and calm. It's a good idea for you to turn to friends and family and talk to them about what you're feeling. They share your pain on some level, especially if they had a great relationship with your dog, too. It will actually make you feel better knowing that someone understands what you're going through and is willing to listen to you unload your emotions.

Moving On

The grief you feel for your dog will pass at some point, and there is no particular timeline you should follow for your grieving process. We all grieve in our own ways, and it may take a month for some people, while others will still be feeling sad about the loss of their dear pet a year after his passing. Just remember, time will eventually heal the pain of losing your beloved pet.

CHAPTER 13

First Aid

You come home to find that your dog just ate a whole chocolate bar or swallowed a chicken bone or is limping. Would you know what to do? It's important to teach yourself basic first aid for dogs in case of an emergency and you're unable to take your dog to the vet immediately. You may be vigilant about his safety, but you can't keep a close eye on him all the time. Accidents do happen, no matter how hard you try to prevent them. So although prevention is important, you should also know what to do in an emergency—just in case. After all, being able to do first aid helps you become a better, more involved dog owner. Hopefully, you will never need to handle any of the situations below, but it never hurts to be prepared. Here are some basic first aid procedures you should perform in various emergencies.

the problem

Your Dog is Bleeding

Blood is oozing from a wound or body opening and the bleeding won't stop.

What to do: Apply pressure using a thick gauze or a towel on the bleeding area. Keep the gauze in place over the wound then wrap it firmly with elastic bandage. Remember that firmly doesn't mean tightly, so just make sure that the bandage is secure. Wrap it too tightly and you could cut off circulation or make the area swell. If your dog is wounded below the elbow, the entire lower leg, including the foot, should be wrapped. Make sure to keep it all in place with adhesive tape. You can also try to elevate your dog's leg if his injury is on the lower part of his body. This is just a temporary fix so your dog's wound isn't exposed and to help stop the bleeding. You should do this until the bleeding stops and you've reached your veterinarian. Get in touch with him or her the moment you spot any bleeding. While you're performing first aid, make sure that your dog is relaxed and calm, and isn't moving around too much.

If your dog is suffering from a nosebleed, apply an ice pack to his muzzle. You're going to need your vet's help in this situation, particularly because nosebleeds aren't common in dogs.

the problem

Your Dog Has Cuts or Scrapes

Shallow cuts are easier to treat and can be done so at home, while serious, deeper ones should be handled carefully.

What to do: Wash the wound with clean water to flush out any dirt and debris. Wipe the wound dry with clean cotton or gauze. Apply a topical antiseptic solution or cream prescribed by your vet twice a day until the cut heals.

Cuts are a normal part of your dog's life, but deeper ones, which may be caused by broken glass or barbed wire, should be taken care of right away. Apply pressure to the bleeding area with a gauze pad or bandage, replacing it once it becomes saturated with blood. Check out the tips above as well for instructions on what to do if your dog is bleeding.

the problem

Your Dog Was in a Car Accident

After being hit by a car, he's hurt, limping, or simply unable to get up.

What to do: Move your dog to a safe place right away, taking care to move him without bending his neck, spine, and legs. As much as possible, find a firm, flat surface to lay your dog on. If you notice that your dog isn't moving or his gums are pale, refrain from moving him around too much. You can also do cardio-pulmonary resuscitation. As always, call your vet to inform him or her about what happened, then bring your dog to the vet.

Remember that your dog may feel uncomfortable after the accident, and there's a chance that the pain will cause him to behave aggressively for a short while. In this case, you need to be careful when approaching him. Putting a muzzle on your dog could keep him from biting you while you're trying to perform first aid. Some dogs may also flee after an accident, which might make you think that your dog isn't severely hurt. Even if your dog seems okay after getting hit, you should still take him to the vet to make sure that he doesn't have any broken bones or internal injuries.

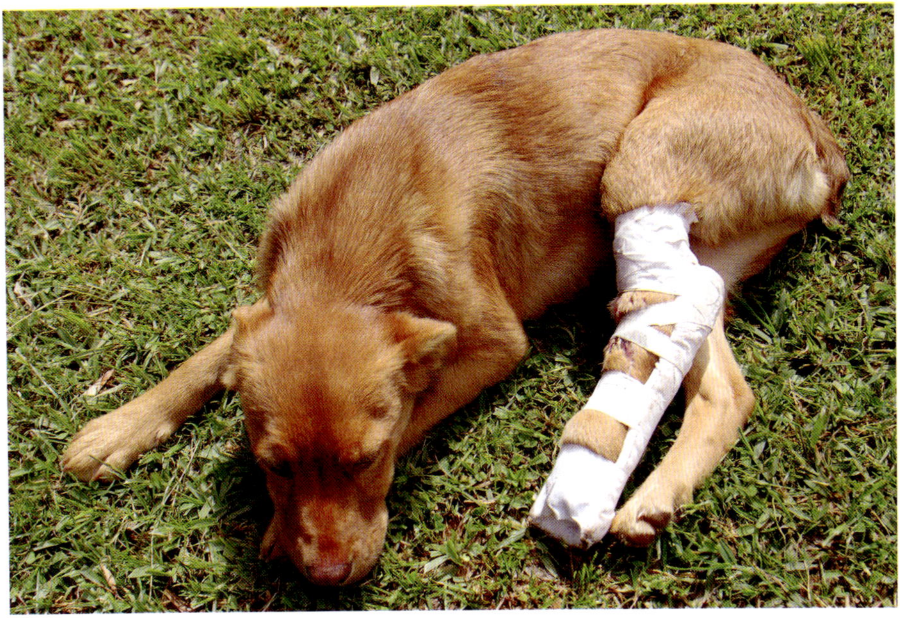

Your Dog Has a Fractured Bone

the problem His leg is broken or is bent at an abnormal angle. He also won't put any weight on it.

What to do: Apply a temporary splint, then wrap the injured limb very carefully with a roll of newspaper to keep it from swinging back and forth. Make sure to secure the ends of the roll of newspaper with tape to keep it from coming undone. Check your dog's leg as well and see if there are any wounds, which you should clean and treat.

If the fracture is too high for you to apply a splint, there are a couple of options you can take depending on the size of your dog. If you have a small dog, place him in a padded box and prevent him from walking. If you have a large dog, he can get around on three legs. Either way, you will need to bring your dog to the vet.

Your Dog Is Not Breathing

the problem You don't see your dog's chest rising or feel air coming out from his nose or mouth. Various situations can cause this, such as near-drowning.

What to do: First, open his mouth, pull his tongue to the side, and see if there is anything obstructing his airway passage. If it is clear, perform artificial respiration. Put his tongue back in place, close his mouth, then blow steadily into your dog's nostrils until you see his chest rising; the amount of air you exhale should depend on the size of your dog. Allow the dog to exhale on his own and listen for a heartbeat. Repeat this six times a minute, and then take him to the vet.

the problem

Your Dog's Heart Has Stopped

You don't feel or hear any heartbeat in his chest.

What to do: Use the external heart massage technique. Set your dog down on his right side on a firm surface. Position your hand on the chest area, directly behind your dog's elbow. Press your hand firmly and release it once every second. Do this six times in a row, wait five seconds to allow the chest to expand first, then repeat the process. Use a moderate amount of pressure so you don't break your dog's ribs. Take a look at his gums as well to see if they've turned pink again. Listen for your dog's heartbeat. Make sure a veterinarian sees your dog immediately.

This technique can be used alternately with artificial respiration in case of cardio-pulmonary failure or when both the heart and breathing stop.

the problem

Your Dog Is Having an Allergic Reaction

In milder cases, he has hives or his face has some swelling. In more severe cases, he is vomiting, drooling, has pale gums, diarrhea, and a fast heart rate.

What to do: If it's just a mild case, let your vet know about it and tell him or her what possibly caused the reaction—whether it's food, insect sting, dust, or even dander—and get advice on how to avoid or deal with it next time. Your vet may prescribe antihistamines for your dog. If he is having a severe allergic reaction, rush him to the vet immediately so steroids can be administered and he can be put on oxygen, among other treatments.

Allergies in dogs are very serious and go well beyond the sneezing and sniffling that afflict humans, especially since dogs wouldn't know how to cope with or treat the allergies. Just remember to stay alert if you notice any changes in your dog's behavior.

the problem

Your Dog Is Having Convulsions or Seizures

Your dog's whole body or his extremities may be stiffening and relaxing alternately.

What to do: First of all, don't restrain your dog. Surround him with towels to keep him comfortable or place him on a padded surface. When he's in place, record the duration and frequency of his seizures. You may need to apply cardio-pulmonary resuscitation if necessary. Make sure to take your dog to the vet right away if he is weak, disoriented, or may have ingested a poison. Your vet should still be involved even if your dog seems normal after one episode. He or she can decide what to do next and if your dog should be examined and treated.

the problem: Your Dog Is Choking

He is pawing at his mouth, gagging, and gasping for air, and his neck is positioned at a strange angle.

What to do: Try to open his mouth and clear the airway. You can do the Heimlich maneuver by pushing up with your fist held up against the dog's belly, just behind the ribcage. Do this firmly, but not with excessive force—you don't want to injure him any further. After you've dislodged whatever he's choking on, take him to the vet immediately.

the problem: Your Dog Has Been Burned

Burns could either be chemical, electrical, or caused by heat.

What to do: Cut off a bit of the fur on the burned area so you can see the skin more clearly. Flush the affected area immediately with cold water, then apply an ice pack wrapped in a towel for five to 10 minutes. Small burns can be treated with an antibiotic cream prescribed by your vet, applied twice daily. But if your dog has bigger burns, second- or third-degree burns, or his skin looks infected, bring him to your vet.

the problem: Your Dog Is Suffering from Heatstroke

Your dog collapses after a long walk or was left out under the sun. Other symptoms include thick saliva, vomiting, excessive panting, and difficulty breathing.

What to do: Bring your pet to a cool, shady area immediately; you can also position him in front of an electric fan. You need to act fast because once your dog's temperature hits 41 degrees Celsius and goes even higher, his internal organs will begin to break down. You can use a rectal thermometer to keep track of his temperature. Give him a bowl of water to help him cool off.

Begin to wet him with tap water, concentrating on the head, chest, belly, armpits, and paws. You can also apply additional ice packs on other parts of his body to cool him down much quicker. Perform cardio-pulmonary resuscitation if needed, and then take him to the vet. Even if he has recovered from the heatstroke, there may still be some damage to his organs, so an immediate checkup is necessary.

the problem

Your Dog Ingested Something Poisonous

Poisoning symptoms include skin rash, diarrhea, vomiting, drooling, and hallucinations (which you can detect if your dog has been overreacting to any sounds or sights). The symptoms may not show up right away and could take at least three days to appear.

What to do: You should take your dog to the vet right away. If this isn't possible just yet, give your dog three percent hydrogen peroxide antiseptic solution. A simple way to figure out how much you should give him is by knowing how much he weighs—your dog would need one to three tablespoons of the solution for every five pounds. A 15-pound dog, for example, can have up to nine tablespoons of the solution. The same rule applies if you are giving him activated charcoal instead. Give him one capsule for every five pounds.

You shouldn't induce vomiting unless your vet tells you to do so or until you know for sure if the poison is an acid, alkali, corrosive, or contains petroleum products. Refrain from inducing vomiting as well if your dog is unconscious or isn't swallowing.

Keep your dog safe next time by putting away chemicals and substances such as insecticides, cleansers, fertilizers, mouthwash, detergents, and bleach. Your medicines and other supplements should also be kept in your medicine cabinet. Some human medicines may be okay for dogs, but some can be toxic, so it's better to be safe than sorry. Food items should also be properly stored to prevent your dog from finding and consuming them.

Applying Eye Drops or Ointment to Your Dog's Eyes

Your dog might need medication for his eyes from time to time, especially if he suffers from dry eyes and other conditions.

1. Prepare the medication.
2. Dip a cotton ball in saline solution and use it to clean your dog's eyes. Use a different cotton ball for each eye to keep from spreading bacteria from one eye to the other.
3. When applying eye drops, tilt your dog's head back and keep his eyes open. Put the bottle as close to the eye as possible, but don't let it touch the eyeball, then squeeze in a few drops. Repeat with the other eye if necessary. Then, you can let your dog go; when he blinks, the solution will spread all over his eyes.
4. When applying ointment, hold your dog's head in place and use your fingers to keep your dog's eyelids open. Squeeze a small amount of ointment onto the eye, then repeat with the other eye if necessary. The medicine will usually spread by itself when your dog blinks, but other dogs may need you to hold their eyes closed—gently, without pressing on his eyeballs—so the medicine will be absorbed more thoroughly.

Giving Medicine to Your Dog

Giving your dog his meds is something you will have to do as part of his treatment after a health emergency or to address any medical issues he has been having. Here are step-by-step tips to giving meds to your dog and making sure he keeps them down.

Giving Liquid Medication

1. Prepare the medication and either a syringe, dropper, or teaspoon.
2. Hold your dog's muzzle closed and tilt it up high.
3. Pour the liquid at the side of your dog's mouth, between the fangs and the molars, while his head is still tilted up.
4. Hold his mouth closed and rub your dog's neck to encourage him to swallow the medicine.

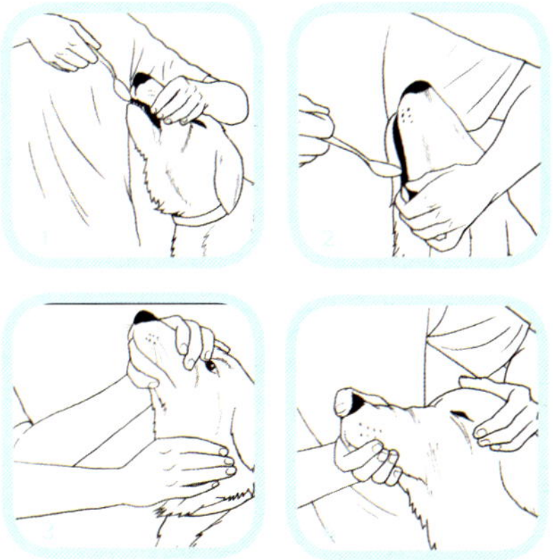

Giving Your Dog a Tablet or Capsule

1. Prepare the medication.
2. Hold your dog's muzzle closed and tilt it up high.
3. Open your dog's mouth carefully, then put the tablet or capsule into his throat, reaching in as far as you can. Make sure his head is still tilted up.
4. Close his mouth and rub his neck to make sure he swallows the pill.

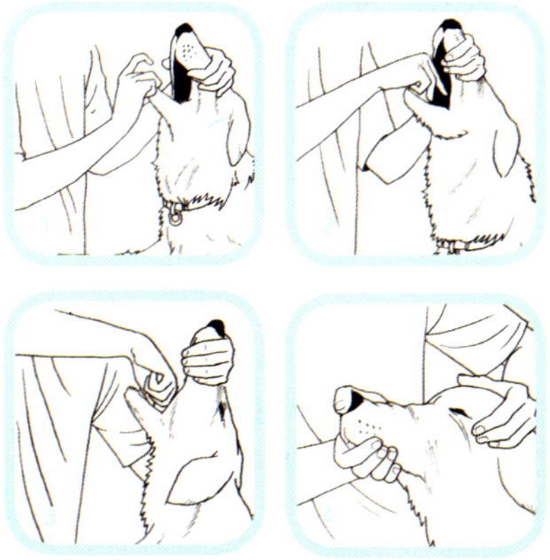

Preparing Your Dog's Emergency Kit

Having an emergency kit can help you respond immediately to any problems that your dog might have, ensuring that you'll have everything you need at hand and ready to use.

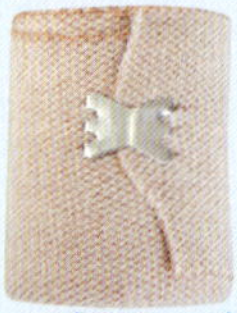

Elastic Bandage and Adhesive Tape

Have these on hand in case your dog has fractures, wrapping the affected limb secure with the bandage and keeping it in place with the tape.

Cotton

This is useful for any purpose, whether it's for cleaning your dog's eyes or his wounds, or for removing any discharge or wax in your dog's ears.

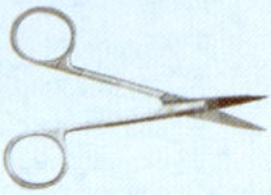

Small Scissors

Use this to cut gauze, bandages, or tape that you may need to dress his wounds.

Gauze

Use this to help apply pressure and to stop any bleeding.

Tweezers

You can pick off any foreign objects from your dog's body and even remove any ticks you may find on his fur.

Saline Solution or Triple-distilled Water

You can use this to clean your dog's wounds or flush out foreign objects from his eyes.

In additional to the items above, you might also want to have a dog book in your emergency kit to walk you through any basic first-aid procedures you might need to perform. Don't forget to include your vet's phone number as well. You might know his or her number by heart, but this information will be useful to anyone else in your household who may need to perform first aid on your dog.

It's definitely a good idea to bring this emergency kit along with you on any trips you will be taking with your dog, just in case any accidents occur or he develops any health issues while you're on the road. Always have your vet's number on hand and find out if there are any vets near the area where you will be staying. Some people also make sure that, along with the emergency kit, they have an easy-to-carry dog survival kit ready to keep their dogs safe, well-fed, and comfortable after natural disasters like typhoons.

Be sure that everyone in your household knows how to administer first aid to your dog in case of emergencies. This gets everyone involved in the care

Small Bowl

Have this ready for your dog to drink water out of, especially in case of heatstroke. You can also use a collapsible bowl to save more space.

Thick Towel

You can use this to cushion your dog or wrap him in it if he needs to be transported safely to the vet.

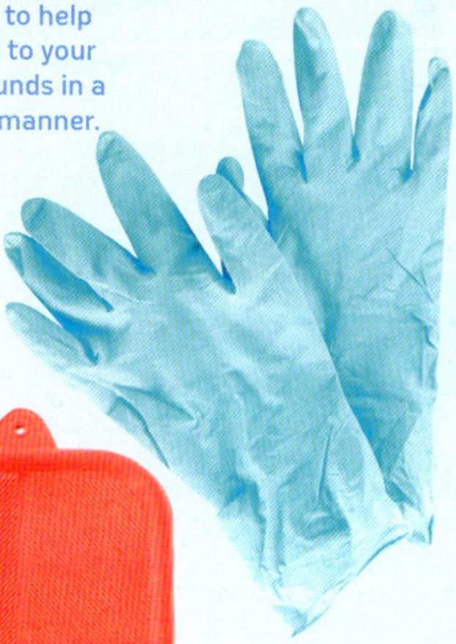

Gloves

Use this to help you tend to your dog's wounds in a sanitary manner.

Antiseptic Solution and/or Cream

You can use this to keep your dog's wounds from getting infected.

Small Flashlight

Use this to look into your dog's mouth to check for obstructions.

Hot Pack

Consider having a hot pack in your kit as well.

of your dog and will ensure that they can handle any possible problems, instead of panicking and just waiting for you to come and help. Teach them the various techniques that can save your dog in different situations, and make sure you leave your vet's number prominently displayed so they can call him or her if there is any problem with your dog and you're not around to handle it.

All of you should also be aware of the location of the nearest veterinary clinic. If your vet is located elsewhere or too far to get to your house quickly, it is better to bring your pet to the closest clinic rather than wait for your vet to arrive. Getting immediate medical attention is better than being too late to save your pet.

Always remember that giving your dog first aid is not a replacement for veterinary attention. Just because you've given your dog first aid doesn't mean you shouldn't call your vet for help or that the problem has been solved. First aid should be done between the time the emergency occurs and the time when you get to the nearest veterinary clinic. Performing first aid can help save your dog's life.

COVER
(Cover Photo) Christian Halili, (Five Dogs) © Erik Lam | Dreamstime.com

ABOUT THE AUTHORS
(Margarita Carpio) Christian Halili, (Jojo Isorena) Ben Lim

INTRODUCTION
(Pomeranian) © Daniel Raustadt | Dreamstime.com

CHAPTER 1
Getting Your First Puppy
Page 6 (Spitz) © Webandblack | Dreamstime.com, Page 11 (Mixed Breed Boomer Dog) © Erik Lam | Dreamstime.com, Page 12 (Labrador Retriever) At Maculangan, Page 13 (Collie) © Sunheyy | Dreamstime.com, (Alaskan Malamute) At Maculangan, Page 14 (Beagle) Vincent Coscolluela, (Miniature Schnauzer) Miguel Miranda, Page 15 (Shih Tzu) At Maculangan, (Lhasa Apso) Dairy Darilag, Page 16 (Small pugs) © Tatiana Morozova | Dreamstime.com, Page 22 (Food bowl) Dakila Angeles, Page 27 (Dog Toilet Training) © Markcarper | Dreamstime.com, Page 32 (Young Papillon) © Sergey Lavrentev | Dreamstime.com, (Red crate) © Vitaly Titox | Dreamstime.com

CHAPTER 2
Understanding Your Dog's Club Certificate
Page 34 (Golden Retriever) At Maculangan, Page 38 (Good Dog Certificate) Grace Marcellana

CHAPTER 3
Nutrition
Page 54 (Dog Dinner Time) © Willeecole | Dreamstime.com, Page 45 (Beagle puppy eating) © Monika Wisniewska | Dreamstime.com, Page 49 (Dog food) Dakila Angeles, (Spoiled dog) © Willeecole | Dreamstime.com

CHAPTER 4
Healthcare
Page 54 (Puppy getting vaccinated) © Willeecole | Dreamstime.com, Page 58 (Chew toy) Vincent Coscolluela, Page 60 (Sleeping Labrador puppy) © Suto Norbert | Dreamstime.com, Page 62 (The sick dog) © Olena Adamenko | Dreamstime.com, Page 65 (Veterinary care) © Willeecole | Dreamstime.com, Page 67 (Sleeping old dog) © Dmccale | Dreamstime.com

CHAPTER 5
Grooming
Page 70 (Toy poodle grooming) © Liuying Lu | Dreamstime.com, Page 72 (Comb) Christian Halili, (Dog likes a shower) © Oleksandr Lishchinskyi | Dreamstime.com, Page 74 (Dental chew) Christian Halili, (Brushing the teeth) © Elisabeth Hammerschmid | Dreamstime.com, Page 75 (Dog's Eye) © Bigzendragon | Dreamstime.com, Page 76 (Sweet scratching puppy) © Amyinlondon | Dreamstime.com (Ear-cleaning illustration) Sonny Ramirez, (Nail illustration) Grace Marcellana, Page 79 (Dog butt) © Valentino Ristevski | Dreamstime.com, Page 80-81 (Dog grooming) © Willeecole | Dreamstime.com

CHAPTER 6
Socialization
Page 84 (Dog Banner) © Stefan Hermans | Dreamstime.com, Page 88 (Hiding Puppy) © Julie Campbell | Dreamstime.com, Page 91 (Chihuahua) © Photobac | Dreamstime.com

CHAPTER 7
Training
Page 94 (Black Bichon playing) © Viorel Sima | Dreamstime.com, Page 97 (Treats) Christian Halili, Pages 98-101 (Jojo Isorena, Brad Feliciano, and dogs) Ben Lim

CHAPTER 8
Exercise and Play
Page 102 (Shih tzu puppy running in grass) © Glenn Nagel | Dreamstime.com, Page 104 (Poodles playing) © Parpalea Catalin | Dreamstime.com, Page 105 (Woman walking dog) © Palms | Dreamstime.com, Page 106 (Funny catching) © Andra Cerar | Dreamstime.com

CHAPTER 9
Travel
Page 108 (Two small puppies in a vintage suitcase) © Sjhuls | Dreamstime.com, 111 (Dog in a car window) © Mathew Hayward | Dreamstime.com, 115 (Dog on beach) © Mathew Hayward | Dreamstime.com

CHAPTER 10
Common Behavior Problems
Page 116 (Cross Breed dog in front of white background) © Isselee | Dreamstime.com, Page 119 (Lizard toy) Christian Halili, Page 120 (Dental chew) Christian Halili

CHAPTER 11
Sexual Maturity and Breeding
Page 124 (Pet dog) © Christopher Waters | Dreamstime.com, Page 127 (Poodle dog staring) © Stockshooter | Dreamstime.com, Page 130 (Jack Russell Terrier puppies) © Erik Lam | Dreamstime.com

CHAPTER 12
The Homestretch
Page 132 (Angel dog) © Annette Shaff | Dreamstime.com, Page 134 (Balloon poodle dog) © Lunamarina | Dreamstime.com, Page 137 (Black Labrador Mix Puppy wearing angel wings) Adogslifephoto | Dreamstime.com

CHAPTER 13
First Aid
Page 138 (Cute Dachshund) © Claucarlsen | Dreamstime.com, Page 141 (Canela) © Marfle | Dreamstime.com, Page 142 (Heart massage illustration) Sonny Ramirez, Page 143 (Giving your dog medicine illustrations) Sonny Ramirez, Page 147 (Hot water pack) © Ambro10 | Dreamstime.com, (Medical Gloves) © Nataliya Kuznetsova | Dreamstime.com, (Gauze, Tweezers, Elastic bandage, Cotton, Antiseptic solution, Thick towel, Small flashlight) Christian Halili, (Credits) Isselee | Dreamstime.com)

BOW & WOW PRODUCTS FEATURED
Page 22 and Page 45 ETH Dog Dish, Page 49 and Page 42 Wellness Complete Health Dry Dog Food Lamb, Page 58, Nylabone Durachew, Page 72 JWP Rotating Comb, Page 74 and Page 118 Zuke's Z-Bones Carrot and Cherry, Page 95 CS Tricky Trainers Treats, Page 117 Kong Braidz Small Gecko

All items are available at
Bow & Wow
5th level Shangri-la Plaza Mall,
EDSA, Mandaluyong City
(632) 638-3372 / 0927-906-8700

Bow & Wow
Lower Ground Floor
Greenbelt 5, Makati City
(632) 501-3681 / 0916-627-7820

VETS IN PRACTICE
63 Maysilo Circle, Plain View (Boni Avenue), Mandaluyong City

BETTERDOG CANINE BEHAVIOR CENTER
Building C, Karrivin Plaza, 2316 Pasong Tamo Extension, Makati City

MARK YOUR CALENDARS!

The cutest furry friends are here to accompany you all throughout 2012!

Grab your copy of Good Dog magazine bundled with Good Housekeeping's April, July, October and December issues for only P125!

GOOD Dog

SUMMIT MEDIA